Kaaterskill Clove

Kaaterskill Clove
Where Nature Met Art
by Raymond Beecher

Published by
Black Dome Press Corp.
1011 Route 296
Hensonville, New York 12439
www.blackdomepress.com
Tel: (518) 734-6357

First Edition Paperback 2004
Copyright © 2004 Greene County Historical Society, Inc.

Without limiting the rights under copyright above, no part of this publication may be reproduced, stored in or introduced into a retrieval system, or transmitted, in any form, by any means (electronic, mechanical, photocopying, recording, or otherwise), without the prior written permission of the publisher of this book.

Library of Congress Cataloging-in-Publication Data
Beecher, Raymond.
Kaaterskill Clove: where nature met art/by Raymond Beecher.—
    1st ed. pbk.
    p. cm.
  Includes bibliographical references and index.
  ISBN 1-883789-41-9
1. Kaaterskill Clove (N.Y.)—History. 2. Kaaterskill Clove Region (N.Y.)
    History. I. Title.

F127.C3B44 2004
974.7'37--dc22
                        2004012173

Front cover: Sanford Robinson Gifford (American, 1823-1880), *A Gorge in the Mountains* (*Kauterskill Clove*), 1862, oil on canvas, 48 x 39 7/8 in. (121.9 x 101.3 cm): The Metropolitan Museum of Art, Bequest of Maria DeWitt Jesup, from the collection of her husband, Morris K. Jesup, 1914 (15.30.62). Photograph © The Metropolitan Museum of Art

Back cover: Alburtus del Orient Browere (1814-1887), *Rip Van Winkle Leaving Home* (detail), 1884, oil on canvas, 24 x 33 in. The Beecher Trust Collection.

Design: Ron Toelke Associates
Printed in the USA

10 9 8 7 6 5 4 3 2 1

Kaaterskill Clove

Where Nature Met Art

Raymond Beecher

Catterskill Falls.
Catskill Mountains, New York, U.S.

"Midst greens and shades the Kauterskill leaps,"
 From cliffs where the wood flower clings,
All summer he moistens his verdant steeps
 With the sweet light spray of the mountain springs;
And he shakes the woods on the mountain side,
 When they drip with the rains of autumn tide." *Bryant.*

⇛ DEDICATION ⇚

A number of individuals and nonprofit groups have maintained over the decades a watchful eye on the preservation of Kaaterskill Clove's scenic beauty, but two individuals—one in the nineteenth century, and one in the twentieth and twenty-first centuries—deserve special accolades. This book is dedicated to E.T. Mason and Justine L. Hommel.

B.B.G. Stone, Catterskill Falls. *Lithograph produced by John H. Bufford, Boston, 1867, with first stanza of William Cullen Bryant's poem* Catterskill Falls. *Fellow artist Sanford Robinson Gifford wrote to Stone, "I have seen a great many pictures of this beautiful spot but I have now seen a more truthful one."*

"Map Showing Summer Resorts among the Catskills," included in the Hudson River Day Line's 1894 *"Summer Excursion Routes"* brochure.

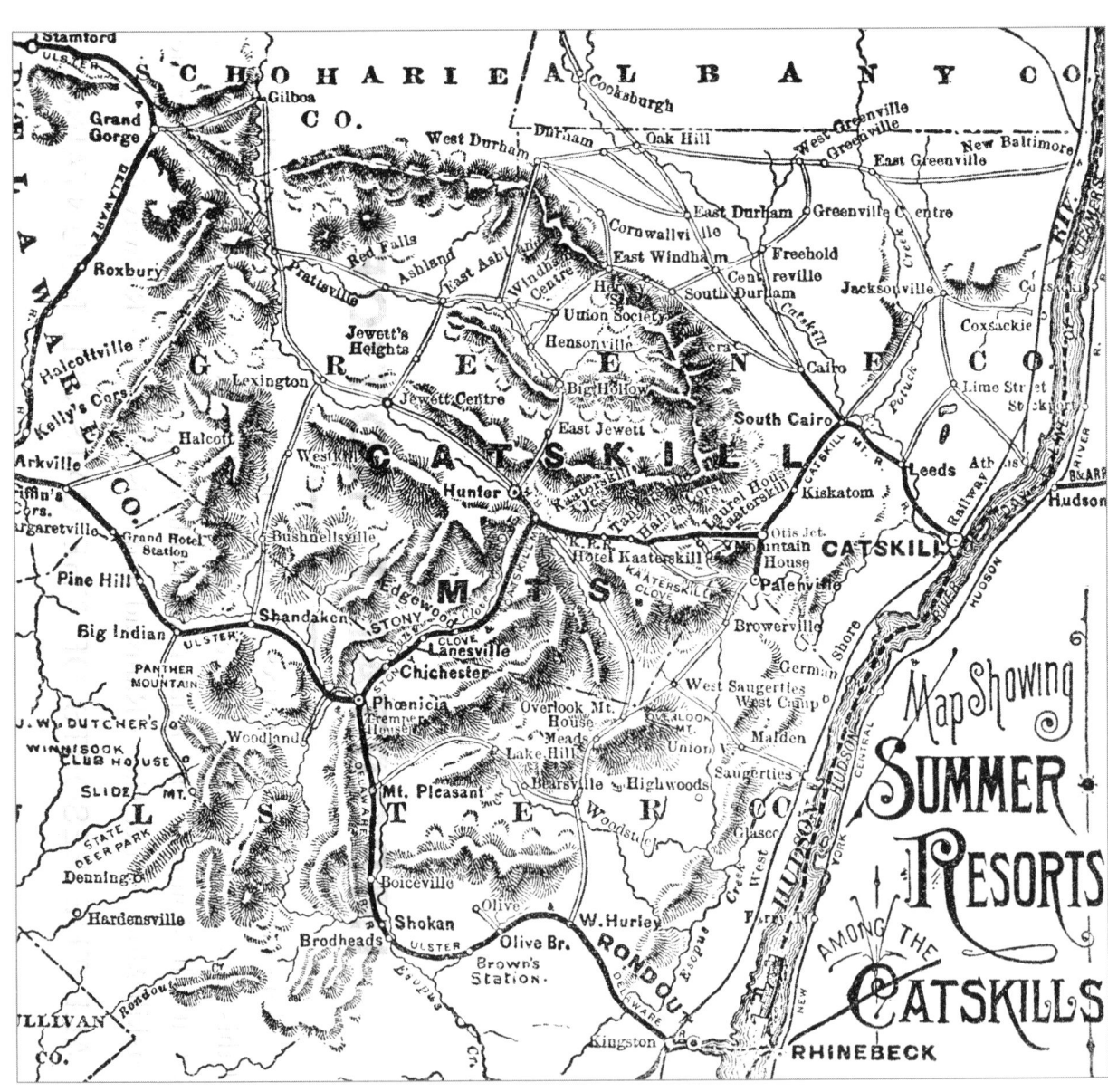

TABLE OF CONTENTS

Foreword	8
Acknowledgments	14
Prologue	16
I. Legend and Lore	**19**
Rip Van Winkle	20
Native Americans	30
II. The Clove in American Art	**35**
Nineteenth-Century Artists in the Clove: The Hudson River School	36
Kindred Spirits	48
Poor Man's Art	52
Stereoscopic Views	58
E.T. Mason, Patron Saint of Kaaterskill Clove	62
B.B.G. Stone (1829-1906), Second Generation of the Hudson River School	68
The Palenville Art Colony	76
Walton Van Loan, "Mr. Catskill"	80
III. Literary Sketches	**91**
European Travel Writers	92
American Writers—Amateur and Professional	96
IV. Grand Hotels and Private Parks	**109**
Summer Guests at the Mountain House, 1880	110
Summer Guests at the Mountain House, 1905	118
Hotel Kaaterskill	126
The Laurel House	136
Guests at the Mountain House, 1922	142
The Mountain House for Sale	146
The Mountain House under Van Wagonen Ownership	154
Mountain House Finale	158
Homes near to Nature	166
V. Harvesting the Clove's Resources	**175**
Industry in the Clove	176
Logging the Pine Orchard	182
South Lake's Ice Crops	188
VI. The Clove Road	**193**
Traveling Kaaterskill Clove	194
The Clove Race that Fizzled Out	198
"Jacob's Ladder" or the "Rip Van Winkle Trail"?	202
Epilogue: Thomas Cole, Cedar Grove, and Kaaterskill Clove	210
About the Author	214
Endnotes	215
Additional Reading	218
Index	219

⇒ FOREWORD ⇐

Kaaterskill Clove, the breathtakingly beautiful ravine between High Peak and South Mountain, is arguably the highlight of the Catskill Park. In *Kaaterskill Clove: Where Nature Met Art*, Raymond Beecher weaves together art, literature, Indian legend, industry and local lore to tell the story of this spectacular mountain gorge. Beecher's knowledge and passion for the history of this sublime section of the Catskills provides readers with a vivid sense of the place and its significance.

In the early 1800s America's search for a national identity led it to focus on what set the United States apart from Europe. Certainly the young country could not compete with the monuments, art and history of hundreds of years of European civilization. Instead, there was this huge wilderness that represented America's potential. Roderic Nash in *Wilderness and the American Mind* identifies "wilderness as the basic ingredient of American civilization." He argues that it is from this wilderness that America is created and that it is the wilderness that defines the country. In 1816, De Witt Clinton, the future governor of New York State summed up the American landscape by saying, "This wild romantic and awful [i.e., inspiring awe] scenery is calculated to produce a corresponding impression on the imagination."

The groundwork for the acceptance and admiration of wilderness in America began in 18th century Europe from a growing interest in landscape. In the early 19th century this interest spread across the Atlantic with European landscape literature and engravings, and was fueled by the poetry of William Cullen Bryant and the watercolors of William Guy Walls's *Hudson River Portfolio* (1821–1825). Americans began to value the landscape experience.

Combined with this heightened appreciation for their native land was a new level of economic prosperity and security that allowed Americans to begin to enjoy leisure travel. But where would they go?

Accessible from the Hudson River, the Catskills became a destination for viewing and experiencing the American wilderness that was promoted by literature and art. Travel books and art helped to popularize the Catskills, and specifically the area of Kaaterskill Clove. Washington Irving's "Legend of Rip Van Winkle" from his *Sketch Book* of 1819–1820 was, according to Irving, set in the Catskills, even though when Irving wrote "Rip Van Winkle" he had only viewed the Catskills from the Hudson River.

The first tourists to the Catskills were drawn to the region of Kaaterskill Clove. Timothy Dwight's *Travels in New England* (1821–22) recognized Kaaterskill Falls and the view from the escarpment as important stops on the American Grand Tour. A combination of factors brought 19th-century visitors to the area. The Catskills were relatively easy to access from New York City, traveling by boat up the Hudson River, or later by train along its shores. By 1825 New York City was the financial and commercial center of the United States and its future as a "world city" was assured. A year-round harbor, a transatlantic port and, with the opening of the Erie Canal, increased access to the interior of the country guaranteed that New York City was a hub for both Americans and visitors.

Local factors also worked towards turning the clove into a destination for travelers. In 1824 the tanning industry brought funds for an improved road through the clove, and in that same year the Catskill Mountain House opened, providing even more than food and lodging to weary travelers—it was also a feature of "the tour." Travelers came to the Mountain House to stay. They marveled at the view from the front porch across the Hudson River to the Berkshires, they fished in North and South Lake, and they ventured to the spectacular Kaaterskill Falls—the highest falls in New York State, standing about 20 feet higher than Niagara Falls.

In the summer of 1825, the young landscape artist Thomas Cole (1801–1848) journeyed up the Hudson River from New York City to the town of Catskill in search of dramatic scenery to paint. That celebrated trip produced three Catskill Mountain scenes and led to his "discovery" as an artist. Cole's early works *Falls of Kaaterskill* (1826) and *The Clove, Catskills* (ca. 1827) illustrate the wild and solitary American landscape that he treasured. They also reflect his love of the region and his numerous ventures to the area of Kaaterskill Clove.

Cole's admiration for the American landscape is a consistent theme in his poetry and essays. On the importance of American wilderness he wrote, "the most distinctive, and perhaps the most impressive, characteristic of American scenery is its wilderness." Cole also argued for "the importance of cultivating a taste for American Scenery."

Cole married Maria Bartow in 1836 and settled in her family home, Cedar Grove. Cedar Grove, by coincidence, has one of the loveliest views across Catskill Creek to the Catskill Mountains, and during Cole's lifetime the view included the Catskill Mountain House, which stood on its rock shelf near the top of Kaaterskill Clove. By 1845 Cole had developed a following of artists who sketched in nature and from those sketches created landscape paintings in his style. This group of artists is now called the Hudson River School and is considered the first American school of painting. The clove became for many Hudson River School artists almost a touchstone; regardless of their other adventures, they often returned to this area to sketch.

In 1844 the aspiring artist Frederic Church would write in anticipation of his studies with Cole: "I have frequently heard of the beautiful and romantic scenery about Catskill ... it would give me the greatest pleasure to accompany you in your rambles about the place, observing nature in all her various appearances." Upon Church's arrival in Catskill, Cole took him on his first sketching trip up Kaaterskill Clove to the Catskill Mountain House. As Cole's foremost pupil, Church followed Cole's lead as shown by his pencil studies of North and South Mountain, and North and South Lake, as well as tree and rock studies and views of the Mountain House that document the clove as one of Church's favorite sketching locations. Using these studies Church created some of his powerful early works, most notably *Above the Clouds at Sunrise* (1849), a dramatic view from the escarpment in front of the Mountain House looking east, in which the foreground rocks, trees and a swirling pink mist give way to a sea of blue clouds. Church's love of the Catskills, instilled by Cole, led Church to build his home, Olana, in such a way and in such a place as to capture spectacular views of the Catskills.

Raymond Beecher's book is perfectly timed. 2004 marks the centennial celebration of the formation of the Catskill Park by Chapter 233 of the New York State Laws of 1904, which established a defined boundary that is commonly referred to as the "Blue Line" (derived from the blue line on official state maps). The process began in 1885 with the protection of the 33,894-acre Forest Preserve in the Catskills, together with 681,374 acres in the Adirondacks, by an amendment to the New York State Constitution. The Adirondacks had been the focus of the amendment; the inclusion of the Catskill land was the result of the last minute efforts of State Assemblyman Cornelius A.J. Hardenbergh. Hardenbergh fought to have Ulster County-owned lands transferred to the state so that the county could avoid paying state tax on the land. He then worked to have Ulster, Sullivan and Greene added to the list of Adirondack counties. Then, in 1894, the Constitutional Convention approved article VII, which stated, "The lands of the state, now owned or here after owned or here after acquired, constituting the Forest Preserve as now fixed by law shall be forever kept as wild forest lands." Though protected, the land was in various detached parcels, and definition was needed to guide further efforts at securing public land. In other words, the "Blue Line" was established to focus future purchases and protection within a specific area.

Today the Catskill Park encompasses 705,500 acres, of which 41 percent is public land—287,000 acres of Forest Preserve—and 59 percent is privately owned land. The beauty of the Catskill Park is that it combines both the "forever wild" areas of mountains for hiking, lakes for swimming, streams for fly fishing, and vistas of forested mountains with working farms and small towns, man and nature coexisting.

Kaaterskill Clove, protected within the "Blue Line," still inspires awe. Visitors frequently pull over at the rest stop near the top of the clove to gaze down the clove or across at High Peak. The more adventurous walk down to Bastion Falls, and then from there hike the half-mile up to Kaaterskill Falls. How many modern visitors to these sites realize that thanks to the creation of the State Park they are enjoying the same hallowed terrain first praised, depicted and celebrated by many of the greatest American writers and artists of the 19th century?

Ray Beecher has dedicated much of his life to preserving the history of Greene County. The culmination of his devotion was his funding of the purchase and initial restoration of Thomas Cole's home, Cedar Grove, in 2000. It is because of his efforts that visitors today enjoy the fabulous view from Cole's porch of the mountains he loved and immortalized. Through his deeds and his writing, Ray Beecher continues to nurture a love of the Catskills in new generations, much in the spirit of Thomas Cole.

Evelyn Trebilcock
Curator, Olana State Historic Site
June 22, 2004

Souvenir photo of Kaaterskill Falls from Samuel E. Rusk's "Foto Factory," Haines Falls, 1890s.

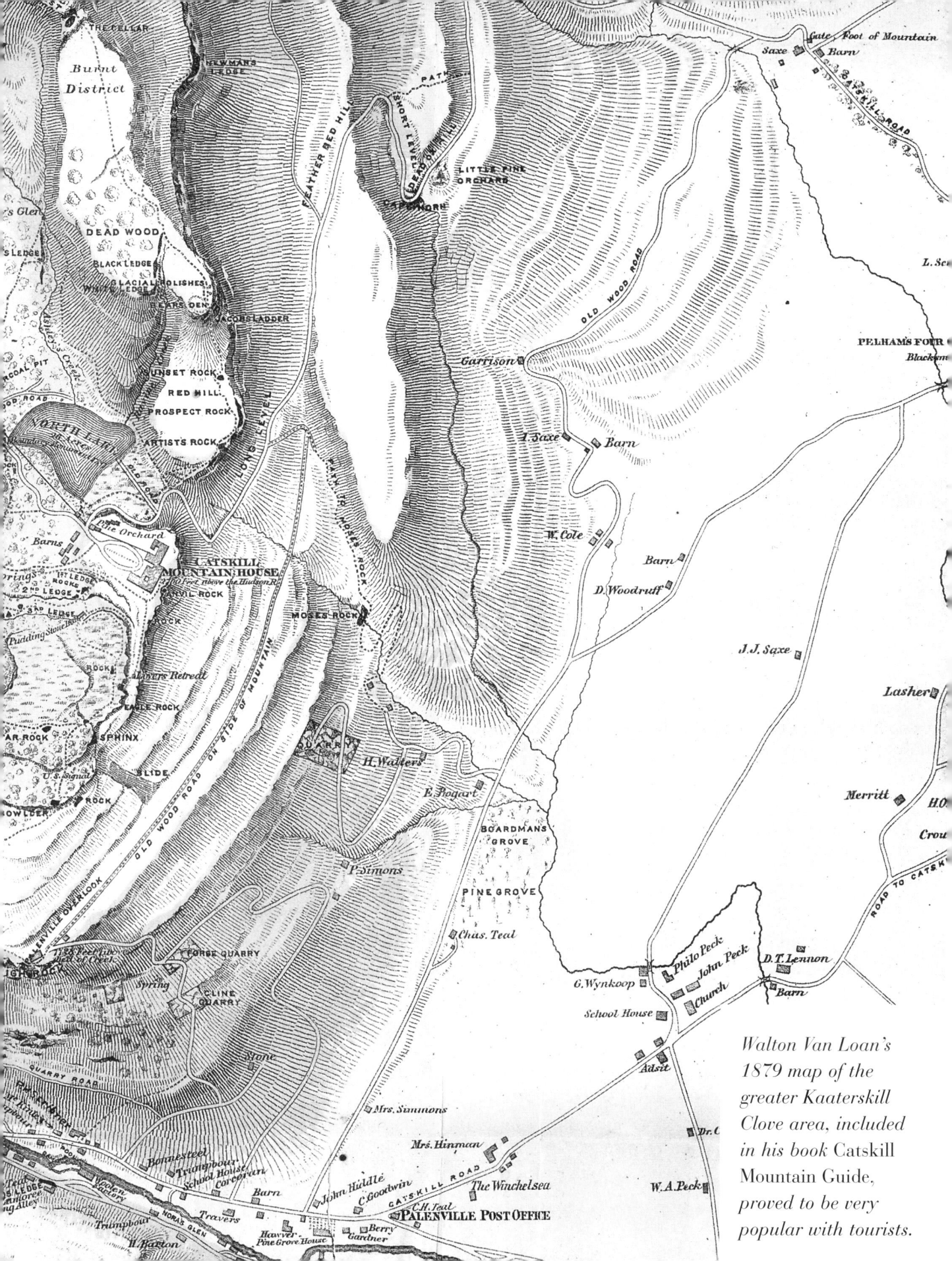

Walton Van Loan's 1879 map of the greater Kaaterskill Clove area, included in his book Catskill Mountain Guide, proved to be very popular with tourists.

ACKNOWLEDGMENTS

The Greene County Historical Society's Vedder Research Library has provided the author with an exceptional opportunity to use both primary and secondary holdings not readily available elsewhere—manuscripts, typescripts, photographs, stereoscopic views, newspapers and long-out-of-print books. Especially helpful in the making of this book were the library's Beach Family Collection, Fiero-Wardle Collection, Rouse Collection, The McCord Collection, B.B.G. Stone Collection, Esther Haines Dunn Memorial Collection, Florence Cole Vincent Memorial Collection, Chadderton Collection, Mabel Parker Smith Collection, and Walter and Dorothy Smith Collection. All illustrations in this book are from the Vedder Research Library's collections unless otherwise noted. The drawings from B.B.G. Stone's sketchbooks, 1854–1867, are of scenes in the Catskill Mountains, but not all are of Kaaterskill Clove.

It was the intent of literary executor Caroline Van Zandt to make her father's Catskill Mountain House and related papers available to future researchers when she officially presented them to the Greene County Historical Society's president Robert Hallock during a Cedar Grove ceremony. This author was among the first to benefit from the Roland Van Zandt Memorial Collection.

From time to time consultation was made with Harvey and Kathleen Durham, who have camped and hiked the Kaaterskill Clove area over the years. They were ever generous of their time and knowledge. I am grateful to Olana State Historic Site Curator Evelyn Trebilcock for penning a fine foreword that adds insights into artist Frederic Church's experience of Kaaterskill Clove, from hiking and sketching with his mentor, Thomas Cole, to intentionally framing the clove like a painting from the windows of his self-designed mansion across the Hudson River from Cedar Grove and the Catskill Mountains.

Justine L. Hommel, the Mountain Top Historical Society, and the Haines Falls Library were most cooperative in sharing Kaaterskill Clove information and the photograph of the Haines quarry on Prospect Mountain. Portions of "When Nature Met Art," this author's essay in the book *Kaaterskill: From the Catskill Mountain House to the Hudson River School*, were combined with new material and reprinted in the chapters "Nineteenth-Century Artists in the Clove" and "Poor Man's Art" with the permission of the Mountain Top Historical Society.

Barbara Smith Rivette has shared in one way or another a body of helpful local history, following in the footsteps of her mother, Mabel Parker Smith, who researched and wrote extensively about Greene County's historical past.

Both Deborah Allen and Steve Hoare of Black Dome Press in their many visits, letters and telephone calls demonstrated endless patience with this Greene County historian and author, over and beyond a publisher's responsibility. Dina Nester rose to the challenge of typing the manuscript from the handwritten pages delivered by age-stiffened hands. Proofreaders Matina Billias, Bob Gildersleeve, Natalie Mortensen, Eric Raetz, and Ed Volmar paid careful attention to the text and made valuable suggestions, and Ron Toelke performed a superb job designing the book.

Kaaterskill Creek at Moore's Bridge. Photograph by J. Loeffler from his Catskill Mountain Scenery series, 1870s.

PROLOGUE

Cleaving the eastern escarpment of the northern Catskills, Kaaterskill Creek—at times a raging torrent, in the drier seasons a placid trickle of water—has created a narrow canyon of singular beauty called Kaaterskill Clove. Artists, poets, writers, photographers and hikers have long admired the clove's scenic splendor. Incorporated in its short distance of four miles are several waterfalls, the two largest being Kaaterskill Falls and Haines Falls.

In the narrowest geographical sense, the name Kaaterskill Clove should be limited to describe the deep ravine bordered by High Peak on the south, and Prospect Mountain and South Mountain on the north. In popular usage, however, the name has come to include a more extended area to the north reaching all of South Mountain, North Lake, the plateau that was the site of the famed Catskill Mountain House, and perhaps beyond.

Nonvolcanic in origin, the Catskill Mountains were born many thousands of years ago as sediment deposited on the bed of a great inland sea that later became subject to upheaval. Erosion gradually cut through the uplifted plateau forming the peaks and soft contours of the mountains we see today. The advances and retreats of glaciers had further erosive impact.

Although much of the clove's water runoff takes the shortest route (eastward) to reach the valley and the Hudson River, a point on the old right-of-way railroad track at Haines Falls divides the water flow, with some descending west and north into the Schoharie basin. With the Kaaterskill's twisting and turning, that water finds itself for a short distance leaving Greene County for adjoining Ulster County, but it soon returns.

The earliest Dutch settlers at Old Catskill (Leeds) and at Kiskatominskauke (Kiskatom) identified this stream of water by words that in translation mean "Male Cats' Kill Creek," or "Tomcats' Creek." The redundancy of "kill" and "creek" is overlooked ("kill" in Dutch means "creek"). Some historians cling to the idea that the name comes from the desire to honor Jacob Katz, poet and Keeper of the Great Seal of the Netherlands.[1] Alf Evers, in his classic volume *The Catskills: From Wilderness to Woodstock*, points out that the English Governor Lord Cornbury disliked Dutch names and sought to identify the Kaaterskill as "Cartwright Creek" in the granting of the Great Hardenbergh Patent.

The spelling of Kaaterskill has several variations. "Cauterskill" was long used in the Hudson Valley. Even noted writer Walton Van Loan used "Cauterskill" in the first printing of his guidebook. Poets and artists in the nineteenth century used

"Catters Kill," "Kauterskill," or "Cats Kills Falls." Today, however, Cauterskill has given way to Kaaterskill except for a geographical district in the town of Catskill and the road by Vedder Mountain.[2]

The story persists that it was George Harding who successfully promoted the spelling as "Kaaterskill" during the building of his Hotel Kaaterskill on South Mountain. It was not beyond Harding to attempt to change place names to promote his hotel. His newspaper publicity reveals he once attempted to change the name of South Mountain to Kaaterskill Mountain.

To the Native Americans of the seventeenth and eighteenth centuries, this wilderness of dense forest and steep inclines had little attraction and was used only as a trail connecting the Hodenosaunee (People of the Long House) in the Mohawk Valley with "the river which flows two ways" (the tidal Hudson River). They came down their trail through the clove to trade in peacetime and to raid during war. They did not use the tortuous edge of the clove's stream itself, but rather a zigzag footpath up South Mountain. This trail was one of the most direct ways to reach Fort Niagara, which was in their British allies' hands after the defeat of the French in Canada during the French and Indian War.[3]

The survival of unique plant specimens in Kaaterskill Clove, particularly in its more inaccessible reaches, is primarily a result of the cold, moist Canadian habitat caused by the clove's generally eastern exposure, steep and rocky terrain, and abbreviated sunlight. George H. Peters, a post-World War II summer sojourner in the valley below the clove, was a keen observer of nature and a skilled hiker. Once, finding it impossible to reach the base of Haines Falls in the upper reaches of the clove, Peters managed to lower himself down the steep drop from the top by means of a sixty-foot length of rope. Continuing down the clove he passed several more cascades and found this to be an ideal climate for plants, especially the rare fragrant shield fern (*Dryopteris fragrans*), which is a survivor from the time of the last retreating glacier.[4]

Benjamin B.G. Stone, pencil drawing of South Mountain looking easterly to the Hudson River Valley.

☙ I ❧
LEGEND AND LORE

While Rip Van Winkle immediately comes to mind as a legend of the Catskills, there are other tales of imaginary and quasi-historical characters associated with the region, many of them centered in Kaaterskill Clove, and Pine Orchard and the eastern escarpment wall (known by Native Americans as "the Wall of Manitou").

Called to the pulpit of the Reformed Dutch Church at Catskill in 1842, the Reverend David Murdock steeped himself in Greene County folklore. The result was the 1861 book, *The Dutch Dominie of the Catskills, or the Times of "Bloody Brant."* Kiskatom's Reverend Charles Rockwell had a similar passion for local legend and published many of them in his book, *The Catskill Mountains and the Region Around: Their Scenery, Legends and History*.

From the sketchbooks of B.B.G. Stone, 1854–1867.

RIP VAN WINKLE

On the evening of July 3, 1835, a young male artist and his hiking companion missed their stagecoach connection. Hiking ten miles, they finally were able to quench their thirst from a common tin dipper left for the convenience of travelers. A few days later the young artist, Thomas Cole, described the eerie experience: "The moon having given way to dark clouds" they reached "a stream leaping from the grand amphitheater of wooded mountains ... dark forests, rugged rocks, towering mountains." He humorously concluded his journal entry by saying that "we did not sleep for twenty years after our potations."

Ever since Washington Irving wrote the legend in *The Sketch Book*, Greene County has claimed Rip Van Winkle as one of its own. Irving was frequently asked as to the actual area in the Catskill Mountains that he had in mind. His reply was, "no particular part." What he didn't tell them was that he had based Rip Van Winkle's long sleep upon several similar folk tales of European origin.[1]

Through the decades Rip Van Winkle has become ubiquitously identified with the region. Rip has lent his name to a bridge across the Hudson River, to social clubs, commercial establishments and festivals. Individuals of an indolent nature are sometimes referred to as "Rip Van Winkle," and Greene County has long called itself "The Land of Rip Van Winkle."[2]

Until the much-improved state road was constructed through the clove from Palenville to Haines Falls, Rip's Hollow had its share of fame as the legendary spot where Irving's Rip Van Winkle met up with a strange individual of short stature overburdened with a filled wooden keg. Since he was of a kindly nature, Rip undertook the task of carrying the keg and thus was led to a wild glen in the depths of the Catskill Mountains. There they joined

C.S. Reinhart's Rip Van Winkle *illustration in Charles Dudley Warner's book* Their Pilgrimage, *Harper & Brothers, 1887.*

LEGEND AND LORE

with an assemblage of odd-looking, dwarfish men playing the game of ninepins. While watching the game, Rip from time to time took an occasional sip from the keg. His senses overpowered him and he fell into a long sleep lasting twenty years. Awakening as an old man, he slowly made his way down the mountain to his village to find the world greatly changed.

Tradition has it that a shanty to provide refreshments for travelers could be found on the Mountain House Turnpike as early as the 1820s. Shortly after the Civil War, a house was built next to it for Ira J. Saxe, who ran it as a summer boardinghouse. William Comfort, formerly of Greene County, alleged in a letter to a newspaper that he built the three-story boardinghouse in 1867. Comfort also alleged that artist Thomas Cole had painted the boardinghouse's sign. (If Cole did so, it must have been for an earlier building; Cole died in 1848. Cole did paint the sign for the Bull's Head Tavern at the foot of Catskill's Jefferson Hill.)

Rip Van Winkle House, a stop along the Mountain Turnpike to the Catskill Mountain House, 1880s.

After a number of years, the building was sold to Mack Haines and then to Gilbert Lusk. During the tenure of the Longfelt family, it burned to the ground. Its final years were a period of inadequate maintenance and the structure deteriorated to almost utter ruin.

In a letter dated March 28, 1984, Thomas H. McCarthy wrote to then-Greene County Historian Mabel Parker Smith and provided information on the property:

> [The building was] rather rambling with a two story porch. My grandfather Robert M. Mabie purchased the property in about 1896 as a summer home for the family. The family never ran it as a business. In 1908 my grandfather passed away and from that time the family ... very seldom used the house being [that] they usually spent from April to July in London and July and August in Newport and Saratoga. The house burned down about 1919. A man by the name of Garrison is thought to be the seller to my grandfather. There were only two levels of land on the 43+ acres—one where the house stood and another round the level of the road where there were stables. Also on the property there is a rather large boulder where some stone cutter cut a figure of Rip Van Winkle. [No one else has made mention of a carved Rip Van Winkle figure on the large boulder. Could McCarthy have been writing about a different location?]
>
> The family often sailed down from Newport to New York and drove up to the house thru Palenville. After grandfather died the place [seemed] so isolated and difficult to keep help. No electricity—a waterfall by the house.[3]

For a time the village of Catskill tried to compete with Palenville as the site of Rip's home. Catskill had some of the quaint buildings described by Irving, but Palenville had the "falling waters" and was sited at the very entrance to Kaaterskill Clove. Palenville seems to have won out, even with actor Joseph Jefferson opting for Catskill.

Joseph Jefferson (1829-1905), an internationally famous actor, described in his autobiography the process by which he adapted the character of Rip Van Winkle to the American stage. While on a summer's vacation (alas in the Poconos, not in the Catskills) he happened to scan Irving's *The Sketch Book*. With a sudden flash of inspiration, he saw the potential for a leading role.[4] Jefferson played Rip to large audiences in New York City's Winter Garden. Later came stock company trips around the United States, Europe, South America, Australia and New Zealand. His London performances were particularly well received.

To Joseph Jefferson's credit, when the village of Catskill's Rip Van Winkle Club asked him to do a one-night solo performance of *Rip Van Winkle* on the stage of the newly constructed Nelida Theater, Jefferson readily agreed. On stage at the Nelida, Jefferson poked gentle fun at the audience and even managed to insert the line "Is this the village of Catskill?" into the last act. It evoked a thunderous round of applause.

That same evening Catskill's Rip Van Winkle Club honored the New York City actor with a reception where he met with local dignitaries and a young man by the name of Nicholas Vedder. The president of the club, nervous with his responsibilities, introduced Joseph Jefferson as "Washington Irving."

As the temperance movement grew stronger in the United States, Joseph Jefferson was urged to adapt *Rip Van Winkle* to promote Prohibition. The Prohibitionists guaranteed full houses for each and every performance if he would refuse the cup of alcoholic beverage offered to him by the character of Gretchen upon his return from his twenty-year sleep. Joseph Jefferson replied, "I would sooner expect to hear Cinderella striking for higher wages or a speech on Woman's Rights from Old Mother Hubbard as to listen to a temperance lecture from Rip Van Winkle."[75]

The famous character was played by three generations of the extended Jefferson family. Joseph's son came to Catskill once a decade. The *Recorder* on November 26, 1909, reported:

> Jefferson here in *Rip Van Winkle*—at the Nelida Theater, at moderate prices on Wednesday evening, December 1st. Manager Lew Fischer yesterday convinced the representative of Jefferson's *Rip Van Winkle* Company that he would get more money in the house on that date at 35 cents, 50 cents, 75 cents and $1 the ticket than if he kept up his usual rates of $1 and $1.50. Mr. Jefferson is bound to fill the Nelida at this scale, for his performance of this masterpiece is easily the event of the season. His last appearance in Catskill was 10 years ago. His famous father opened the Nelida in the same character. ... That play has become one of the classics of the American stage.

Photo presented to B.B.G. Stone by Joseph Jefferson in Catskill, 1887, when Jefferson appeared as Rip Van Winkle at the Nelida Theater.

At about the same time a letter came from Dazey, North Dakota, reporting the finding there of a descendant of former Catskill resident Rip Van Winkle. This Mr. Winkle was then sixty-one years of age and alleged that his grandfather was accustomed to smoking his long Holland pipe and sleeping in his armchair after dinner. The grandfather was a fast friend of Washington Irving, who once told him that he was going to publish a story about him. For those wanting the North Dakotan's signature, they had only to send a self-addressed stamped envelope.

In November 1911, England's London Playhouse was alerting the public that a version of Rip Van Winkle would soon be returning to the English stage. An American admirer of *Rip Van Winkle* commented in the correspondence column of the *London Evening Times:*

> I was amused and interested the other day when I read the announcement outside the Playhouse that Rip Van Winkle is soon to return after a somewhat extended sleep. The notice pleased me for Rip is ever a welcome visitor and is always greeted by the average theater goers, for we all love the little gray man of the Catskills. I say Catskills for that is the American corruption of the ancient word. The bulletin outside the Playhouse says it is a legend of the Katshills. Now nature decreed I should be born within a stone's throw of Rip's mythical residence and so Rip and his mystical haunts are somewhat familiar to me. Rip didn't sleep in the Catskills nor in the Katshills but the Kaathills and undoubtedly he would greatly object to the various corruptions were he now alive. Kaathills was the old original Dutch name—Catskill is the American corruption and Katshill—well that must be the Charing Cross version.

Unfortunately the letter writer's name was not given.

Once, as a civic gesture in support of village improvements, a group of Palenville sojourners persuaded the actor George Ober and a few of his road company to put on an open-air production of *Rip Van Winkle*. So many tickets were sold to Catskill families that the show required a special Catskill Mountain Railway train.

Rips' Rock, a 19th-century tourist attraction near the Rip Van Winkle House and Souvenir Stand.

After World War II the idea was proposed to stage *Rip Van Winkle* as a continuous seasonal production, similar to today's outdoor dramatization of the lost colony of Roanoke, Virginia. Music was written and a Greene County site selected, but, alas, funding did not become available.

The character of Rip Van Winkle intrigued artists of the nineteenth century, and they produced numerous oil paintings and drawings. Of special note are the ones produced by Felix Octavius Carr Darley (1822-1888) for the 1848 American Art Union's edi-

LEGEND AND LORE

tion of *Rip Van Winkle*. Darley was a National Academy exhibitor in 1845 and was once acquainted with Thomas Cole. Darley earned wide popularity as an illustrator for the writings of Washington Irving and James Fenimore Cooper. (A set of Darley's *Rip Van Winkle* illustrations have been on display in the Kaaterskill Clove Gallery at Thomas Cole's Cedar Grove.)

Two coaches costing $675 each were ordered from Abbot-Downing Company, Concord, New Hampshire, in January 1873 and were first used for the 1873 season transporting passengers from Catskill Point to the Beach Mountain House.

A.D.O. Browere (1814-1887), long connected with the village of Catskill, produced several oil paintings of Rip Van Winkle. One set includes: Rip at the village tavern watching his wife scold his drinking cronies; Rip slinking away from home as his wife flourishes a broom; Rip and his dog in the Catskill Mountains wilderness; and Rip in his twenty-year sleep, having aged into an old man. This may be the set once owned by the artist's daughter, Mrs. Frank Van Benschoten of Hudson, New York, and eventually purchased by noted art collector Maxim Karolik. Greene County Historian Mabel Parker Smith once tried to borrow the four oils from Karolik for a show in Catskill, but the effort was unsuccessful.[6]

Of note also is artist Charles Harold Davis's painting, *Rip Van Winkle Returns*. Davis's brush depicts the bewildered old man in tattered clothing, with white hair and beard, leaning against the front door of the ruins of his cottage.

As early as 1829 John Quidor produced a large, 39 1/2-by-49 1/2-inch canvas titled *The Return of Rip Van Winkle*. This folk-art piece now hangs in the Andrew Mellon Collection at the National Gallery of Art in Washington, D.C.

John Roger's groups of statuary cast in bronze also were produced in plaster and a putty color. Included in these "parlor groups" were at least two on the *Rip Van Winkle* theme.

"Rip's Retreat" was built in 1954 near the Mountain House site at Haines Falls. It was advertised as an educational experience for the entire family. Anglo-Dutch architecture was the backdrop for a puppet theater performing Irving's work. Children could play at ninepins on the bowling green, and families could meet old Rip himself for a photo opportunity. The commercial effort was unsuccessful.

Today as each new generation learns the Rip Van Winkle legend, Greene County remains identified as "The Land of Rip Van Winkle."

From the sketchbooks of B.B.G. Stone, 1854–1867.

NATIVE AMERICANS

The "Table Rock" in the Pine Orchard was the geographic background for the "Legend of Lotowana," which appeared in Beers's *History of Greene County* in 1884. According to the legend a Native American chief, Shandaken, camped during the summer at the Pine Orchard with his only daughter, the beautiful Lotowana. Lotowana was much sought after in marriage and was promised to a young Mohawk chief, but Norsereddin, an unprincipled Indian, was determined to secure Lotowana for himself. Norsereddin also was excited by the prospect of winning a 1,000 gold crown marriage bet he had made with a Dutchman.

Norsereddin was rejected by the old chief as a suitor for the hand of his daughter. The renegade struck down the chief and was driven from the summer camp. At the tribal marriage ceremony the chief passed on a gift box to his daughter. Upon opening it Lotowana was fatally bitten by a poisonous snake placed therein by Norsereddin.

Some twenty warriors on horses chased after the culprit and captured him near the Kalkberg. Norsereddin was brought back to the flat rock at the Pine Orchard, where he was burned alive just a few feet from the precipice. His ashes were left on the rock, while Lotowana's body was buried nearby. Shandaken never returned to the site, but his name lives on in neighboring Ulster County.

"View up the Stream from Clove Road Bridge." Photograph by J. Loeffler from the third series of Catskill Mountain Scenery, c. 1870s. Note that Loeffler does not identify the site as Moore's Bridge.

LEGEND AND LORE

Delaware County's Mount Utsayantha, near Stamford, is burdened with a similar tragic legend. The story goes that an American Indian maiden threw herself to her death from a cliff rather than accept an unwanted suitor. Such stories were good promotional material with which to attract tourists in less sophisticated eras.

Writing under the pseudonym, Diedrich Knickerbocker, Washington Irving is responsible for such early-nineteenth-century legends as the aged squaw who controlled the weather, and the mischievous spirit who took the form of wild animals to lead Native American hunters on wild chases through field and forest. Then there is the tale of the hunter who was lost in the mountains, came to Manitou's Rock, and carelessly dropped a gourd from which gushed forth a stream that became the "Katers-kill." The sudden flow of water drowned the hunter.

"High Peak and Round Top." Photograph by J. Loeffler from his Catskill Mountain Scenery series, 1870s. The clove's untamed wilderness would have appeared much like this in the pre-colonial period.

Native Americans

Stereoview taken in "Kauterskill Glen." Printed on the reverse is a quotation from Washington Irving about the Manitou (or spirit), which so bedeviled the Native Americans.

B.B.G. Stone, Looking down the Clove from Haines Falls, *pencil drawing dated September 12, 1854. This scene was immortalized on canvas by Asher B. Durand's* Kaaterskill Clove, *1866, and Thomas Cole's* The Clove, Catskills, *1827.*

II
THE CLOVE IN AMERICAN ART

Nineteenth-century American landscape painters found some of their earliest inspiration in the rugged scenic beauty of Kaaterskill Clove. The clove was the epicenter of America's first homegrown art movement, which came to be known as the Hudson River School (at first derisively).

While paintings of Kaaterskill Clove adorned gallery walls, engravings and drawings of the clove illustrated travel books and magazines such as *Harpers*, *Family Circle*, and *Lippincott's*. These "mass market" publications spread the fame of Kaaterskill Clove and attracted ever more artists and tourists to the region. Some of the clove's most popular attractions—like Kaaterskill Falls and the Catskill Mountain House—were depicted so often that they became American icons. Roland Van Zandt, writing of the Mountain House, noted that "perhaps only the mighty Niagara Falls or the famous battlements of West Point were more familiar to the 19th-century American."

While American painting has passed through many successive stages of artistic inspiration and interpretation since Thomas Cole and the Hudson River School's time, Kaaterskill Clove continues its hold on the imagination of contemporary artists. Efforts are underway to create the Artists' Trail, which will link and interpret many of the sites of most importance to these great nineteenth-century American artists, and Kaaterskill Clove is an essential part of that trail.

From the sketchbooks of B.B.G. Stone, 1854–1867.

Nineteenth-Century Artists in the Clove: The Hudson River School

They were a generation that sketched in the outdoors in the better months of the year. Their sketchbooks were filled with penciled outlines of scenic vistas and margin notes. Returning to their winter studios they translated their sketchbook pages into canvases of exceptional interest. Today their paintings command high prices when they appear on the market, but in the decades of their creation many of the young artists found limited encouragement. An occasional art patron, such as Luman Reed who commissioned paintings from Thomas Cole, was of significant assistance.[1]

They ventured from near and far to the landscape they considered to be "the heart of the Catskills"—Kaaterskill Clove and environs. In this one small corner of the mountaintop were to be found those aspects of American landscape that appealed so strongly to the nineteenth-century artists—a dramatic vista

Nineteenth-Century Artists in the Clove — The Hudson River School

Thomas Cole (1801-1848), The Clove, Catskills, *ca. 1827, oil on canvas, 25 by 36 in. New Britain Museum of American Art, New Britain, CT, Charles F. Smith Fund. Photograph by E. Irving Blomstrann.*

THE CLOVE IN AMERICAN ART

Jacob Ward, Wolf in the Glen (Caterskill Falls), *ca.1825-1826, oil on canvas, 28" by 36". Wadsworth Atheneum, Hartford. Gift of Mrs. Philip G. Stratton. This work was originally thought to be a Thomas Cole painting.*
Jacob C. Ward (1809-1891) was an American landscape painter, illustrator, and pioneer daguerreotypist.

stretching in a wide arc including the mid-Hudson River Valley and easterly into New England, spectacularly beautiful. Here also were to be found two small wilderness-like lakes, draining for a short distance and then plunging abruptly down one of the highest waterfalls in the eastern United States. And there was a fantastic manmade edifice, the Catskill Mountain House, so dramatically situated in the midst of this scenic paradise.

By the end of the nineteenth century, many paintings of what had come to be known as the Hudson River School of Landscape Painting were considered passé and relegated to storage. A revival in interest came after World War II, and by the last two decades of the twentieth century such canvases were being reexamined and revalued. In recent years even the European skeptics have changed their attitudes, as evidenced by a major exhibit of Hudson River School paintings in London. The publishing world lately has produced a number of illustrated volumes of scholarly value. The Hudson River School has assumed its well-deserved place in the history of American art as has Thomas Cole (1801-1848), its "founder."[2]

Until the New England seashore and the American West attracted artists away from the Catskills, many followed Cole's first sketching trip in 1825 to the Kaaterskill Clove section of the northern Catskills. While some Cole dates are conjectural, art historians credit *Lake with Dead Trees* (Allen Memorial Art Museum, Oberlin College) with being among the three oil paintings that resulted from Cole's first trip. That South Lake scene, modified by symbolic tree images, was a milestone in American art.

From that same sketching expedition came *Cascade in Catskill Mountains* (Wadsworth Athenaeum), a view from the mouth of the amphitheater behind the first tier of Kaaterskill Falls. Here the depiction is enhanced with shades of light reflected in water, and with clouds, dark pines, and colorful autumn foliage. Cole sold that original work to John Trumbull and produced a copy, labeled *Kaaterskill Falls*. In 1831 Fenner Sears & Company of London published its engraving *The Falls of Catskill, New York* based upon this Cole oil painting on canvas.

From the Top of Kaaterskill Falls (Detroit Institute of Art) and *Falls of the Kaaterskill* (Warner Collection, Gulf States Paper

Corporation) were painted by Cole in 1826. *In Falls of the Kaaterskill* Cole sought to provide the viewer with a sense of the unspoiled wilderness, while a lone Native American figure adds scale to the natural landscape. Matthew Baigell, in his volume *Thomas Cole*, credits Haines Falls as the subject of this painting, but any hiker familiar with the clove knows that it is Kaaterskill Falls that is depicted. The confusion may be because of the creek names. Haines Falls is, indeed, on the Kaaterskill, while Kaaterskill Falls is located on Lake Creek. Until later in the century when stairs were constructed at Haines Falls that provided ready access from the summit, few travelers and artists undertook the hazardous climb to the base of Haines Falls. *Falls of the Kaaterskill* was originally owned by Cole's friend, poet William Cullen Bryant.

The years 1827-1828 were productive ones for Cole. This period of time brought about the completion of *The Clove, Catskills* (New Britain Museum of American Art) and *The Last of the Mohicans.* The latter painting, based on James Fenimore Cooper's American pioneer novel, depicts the reinterpreted site of the Catskill Mountain House ledge. Almost identical canvases of this work are held by the New York Historical Association and by the Wadsworth Athenaeum.

Just how early in his painting career Cole sought to include the newly-constructed Catskill Mountain House in his sketches is uncertain, but certainly it was within five years of the structure's appearance. *View of the Catskill Mountain House, New York 1828* reveals that hostelry as seen from the tortuous road to the Pine Orchard. It is this familiar scene that was engraved for *History and Topography of the United States.* Enoch Wood, the Staffordshire potter, copied the engraving for his decorated earthenware produced primarily for the American market. This same general area of ascent to the Mountain Top, including the hotel, also appears in an undated Cole production. In this work, he made use of autumn hues and South Mountain.

In 1843 after extensive traveling, Cole again turned to the mountaintop to paint *Catskill Mountain House* (Stillman Collection). Field sketches of this North Mountain view survive in the Princeton University Art Museum. The following year he created *A View of the Two Lakes and Mountain House, Catskill Mountains, Morning 1844* (Brooklyn Museum).

The use of allegorical themes mixed with landscapes was an early product of Thomas Cole's brush, but he had far more difficulty in selling such paintings than the purer landscapes. The same could be said of Cole's contemporaries. In his comparatively short lifetime, even after sketching expeditions throughout the Northeast and his two trips to Europe, Cole never lost interest in his beloved Catskills. Cedar Grove, the Thomson-Cole residence, held the Catskill range in

Nineteenth-Century Artists in the Clove — The Hudson River School

Fawn's Leap, named for a legend of a fawn's fatal attempt to follow its mother in a leap across the chasm. It was the type of legend that appealed to the romantic sensibility of 19th-century travelers. Postcard c. 1905.

sight, with North and South mountains and the Catskill Mountain House foremost in view. Scenes in the Catskill Valley from his brush often used this view for background.

The fact that the panoramic view from North Mountain encompassing the now-famous hotel and the two picturesque lakes was a favorite of Cole's did not deter either Jasper F. Cropsey (1823-1900) or Sanford Robinson Gifford (1823-1880) from repeat performances. A comparison of their efforts is unavoidable. Cole featured a hiker standing in the foreground where twisted, stunted, dead trees barely survive in a harsh environment. In one painting Cole makes use of storm clouds, adding dramatic effect. Jasper Cropsey, in his 1855 oil on canvas entitled *Catskill Mountain House from North Mountain* (Minneapolis Institute of Arts), provides the viewer with a sharper focus. Gone is the human figure, but a dead or dying tree remains.

Cropsey made Cedar Grove a place of pilgrimage after Cole's death, calling on Mrs. Cole and remaining overnight. He would later write of that pilgrimage.

Asher B. Durand, Kaaterskill Clove, *1866, oil on canvas. The Century Association, New York.*

Nineteenth-Century Artists in the Clove — The Hudson River School

Like Cole, Sanford Gifford traveled extensively both in America and abroad, but drew heavily on the Catskill Mountains for his inspiration. Roland Van Zandt, in *The Catskill Mountain House*, succinctly summarized Gifford's admiration: "How important the Catskills were to Gifford may be seen by the Metropolitan Museum of Art's 'Memorial Catalogue' of his work which was printed the year after his death. More than a hundred of the paintings and sketches listed in that catalogue were done in the Catskills, and the majority were painted within a four-mile radius of the Catskill Mountain House."

Gifford's canvas *Catskill Mountains*, produced in 1868, depicts the North Mountain foreground with reduced coverage of the lake, but with an expanded distant view to the southeast. The Mountain House is a small image in this larger scene. An earlier Gifford painting in 1862, *Catskill Mountain House* (Austin Arts Center of Trinity College, Hartford, Connecticut) used much the same perspective.

After Gifford's death, Worthington Whittredge was one of several people to speak about the deceased artist at a meeting of the Century Club on November 19, 1880. Whittredge's explanation of the reason that Gifford became a professional artist bears mentioning. Gifford was a Brown University scholar. After returning to his parental home at Hudson, New York, and somewhat unsure about an adult career, Gifford hiked to the top of Mount Merino early one morning. Resting under a tree, he sat reflecting on the scenic beauty before him as the rising sun reflected its rays on the houses and roofs of the village of Catskill across the Hudson River. "There was one house standing in the village which was in full view, around which we may well believe there was a halo of light that morning which lighted up the path he was to follow," Whittredge said. "This was the house and studio of Thomas Cole, the father of a long line of American landscape painters."

Whittredge continued:

> Many years ago he sought out a little house in Kaaterskill Clove, in which lived a family of plain country folk, and, as the place was secluded and there were no boarders he liked it and managed to obtain quarters there. This house,

THE CLOVE IN AMERICAN ART

Haines Falls in winter, 1890s. Thomas Cole remarked that few visitors to the clove ever saw the wintertime beauty he admired.

scarcely large enough to hold the family, was, nevertheless, for many summers the abiding place of a congregation of artists. The beds were few and it may truly be said that the best were the cheapest, for the most expensive were composed of straw, while the cheapest were of feathers. As may well be imagined, the table at the house was not very good. Gifford was no gourmet, but he had a commendable ambition to improve the cooking of the Catskills. To this end, he urged the immigration of some of the wives and daughters of those present, whose culinary gifts he was acquainted with. In due time they appeared upon the scene and by their adroit direction, new dishes were served and the coffee improved. But this experiment proved fatal in the end. Boarders came in flocks from the city, and Scribner's Boarding House had to be abandoned by the artists and new quarters found further on.

Decade by decade the nineteenth-century artists made the pilgrimage to Kaaterskill Clove. Noted artist DeWitt Clinton Boutelle produced an oil painting of the Mountain House, and in 1849 a group of younger artists—David Johnson, John W. Casilear (1811-1893) and John F. Kensett (1816-1872)—could be found sketching in the clove. On the back of a surviving oil sketch of Haines Falls by David Johnson is the inscription, "My first study in Nature," followed by the names of his two sketching companions. DeWitt Clinton Boutelle painted this two-level aspect in 1845. Sarah Cole, Thomas's sister, painted *Beach Mountain House* (Albany Institute of History and Art), which was inspired by her brother's painting of the famed hotel. In 1866 Asher B. Durand painted *Kaaterskill Clove* (Century Club).

The Honolulu Academy of Arts has Irish-born William Guy Walls's *After 1864* and *Cauterskill Falls on the Catskill Mountains*. Wall painted in the English watercolorist tradition and earned very favorable reviews for *Cauterskill Falls* when it was exhibited at the National Academy of Design in 1827. It is said that Wall's art, which was well received by collectors, was credited with encouraging American artists to seek inspiration at home rather than finding subject matter abroad.

B.B.G. (Benjamin Bellows Grant) Stone first appears upriver at Catskill in September 1851. His diary for that year reveals that he sketched in the Mountain House environs. The following summer, he again used the village of Catskill for his base of operations, frequently walking to Palenville, a distance of approximately eleven miles. Landscape drawing became Stone's primary interest for the remainder of his life.

Several lithographic prints were produced from Stone's drawings. Of particular interest is *Catskill Mountain House*, produced by J. H. Bufford of Boston in 1860. In later years a number of Stone's sketches provided an artistic touch to Lionel DeLisser's *Picturesque Catskills*. Among them were: *Under Sunset Rock, South Mountain; Cliff on South Mountain;* and *Fairy Spring, South Mountain.* Kaaterskill Falls and Bastion Falls also received his attention. Stone's distinctive identification on these sketches is an "S" with a "T" superimposed.

In 1873 at the great art sale of John F. Kensett pictures in New York City, the landscapes of Catskill Mountains scenery brought the highest prices. Among the lot were: *Study of a Tree, Catskill Mountain*, selling for $310; *Reminiscences of Cole*, $265; *Study in Kaaterskill Clove, Catskill Mountains*, $300; *Border of a Brook, Catskill*, $210; and *Haines Falls, Kaaterskill Clove*, $600.

The 1880s found many painters elsewhere than in the Catskill Mountains. But E. Heinmann did *View from Prospect Rock—Kaaterskill Falls*, which was engraved by Searing for *The Land of Rip Van Winkle*. And finally, in 1883, there was Walter Launt Palmer's *Rear View of Mountain House.*

Through the decades Frederic E. Church (1826-1900), first as a pupil of Cole and later as a well-established artist, used the northern Catskills as his subject, with the views from his Columbia County mansion, Olana, a frequent inspiration.

Other artists appeared and reappeared as the decades of the nineteenth century moved onward. Some artists came to view, while others came to sketch and paint. The Palenville Art Colony, a yearly summer gathering of kindred spirits, had a lengthy history during the nineteenth century. Depending upon their lengths of stay and their financial resources, a variety of accommodations were available to these Hudson River artists and their successors.

The Catskill Mountain House after 1823 was one of the more convenient places for food and lodging, although its short season had its drawbacks. Some preferred the Laurel House, practically atop of Kaaterskill Falls, while Brockett's in the Clove was a pre-Civil War facility. Few brought their families, although there were numerous farmsteads in the Kiskatom Valley willing to provide necessities at affordable prices.

The passage of time has brought about the loss of the Catskill Mountain House, and the twin lakes have been combined into one single body of water. Yet much of this mountaintop remains—the hiker superseding the artist, the campground the hotel. Scattered throughout the various states from the Atlantic Coast to Hawaii, in museums, art galleries, and in private collections, is prominently displayed the scenic grandeur of Kaaterskill Clove. It is an American heritage nonpareil.

From the sketchbooks of B.B.G. Stone, 1854–1867.

KINDRED SPIRITS

Few men held a deeper admiration for Thomas Cole than did fellow artist Asher B. Durand (1796-1886), who outlived Cole by many years.[1] Durand was one of the first to discover the work of the then-obscure painter, and their acquaintanceship developed into a lifelong friendship. Following the February 1848 death of Cole, mercantilist and art patron Jonathan Sturgis commissioned Durand to paint a tribute to another deep friendship—between poet and nature lover William Cullen Bryant (1794-1878) and Cole. Durand produced a 44-by-36-inch canvas with the title *Kindred Spirits*. It hangs today in the New York Public Library, a gift to that institution by Bryant's daughter.

The brush of Durand produced a canvas fraught with allegorical significance. Cole and Bryant stand on a rocky ledge overlooking a clove in the Catskills with a waterfall in the distance. To this day the debate goes on: is it Kaaterskill Clove or Plattekill Clove? Writer Alf Evers and photographer Mark McCarroll favor Plattekill Clove, while in past decades Mabel Parker Smith made a strong research case for Kaaterskill Clove, as have others. And there is the third opinion that it is a composite. (After all, Cole promoted the idea that "nature seldom makes a perfect composition.")

Durand spent quite a lot of time in Palenville. It was during his October 1848 sketching trip that he recorded his impressions of "Catskill Clove" as a place "rich

Asher B. Durand, Kindred Spirits, 1849, oil on canvas. Collections of the New York Public Library; Astor, Lenox and Tilden Foundations.

Mabel Parker Smith, the second official Greene County Historian. This photograph by her husband, Lester R. Smith, shows Mabel at the top of the Otis incline on July 4, 1926. Courtesy of Barbara Smith Rivette.

in beautiful wilderness beyond all we have met heretofore." That month he also visited the Catskill Mountain House.

In 1972-73 the staff at the New York Public Library exhibited, just below *Kindred Spirits*, a letter written by Cole to Bryant reporting the former's discovery of the scenic beauty of Plattekill Clove. That letter invited Bryant upriver to see this wealth of nature. Also invited was Mrs. Bryant, "whom Mrs. Cole would be delighted to see again." The letter lends weight to the identification of Plattekill Clove as the location for *Kindred Spirits*.

In February of 1973, Mabel Parker Smith, a strong supporter of Kaaterskill Clove as the inspiration for the painting, arranged a meeting with Donald Anderle, then the chief of the Art Division of the New York Public Library. At that time Anderle stated that it was not the intent of the library staff to make the claim for

Plattekill Clove. His letter of February 14, 1973, in the Mabel Parker Smith Collection at the Vedder Research Library reads:

> In reviewing the Durand file, I came across a copy of a reference letter written by a former Chief of this Division. Its conclusions were based upon a very thorough research of the literature on the artist and relevant manuscript holdings from the Library's collections. Its conclusions are tentative, of course, but unless I am mistaken, your ideas about the geography of the setting seem to fit very well with our assumptions. I was particularly struck by John Durand's phrase "landscape ideal" which came to mind immediately I read your remarks about the cliffs on the right of the picture. [John Durand had used the phrase in his biography of his father published in 1894.]

The Erpf Gallery of the Catskill Center in a recent, juried show, Landscapes by Platte Clove Artists in Residence, included an illustration of *Kindred Spirits* on its printed announcement and stated: "*Kindred Spirits* by Asher B. Durand, the best known of all the clove paintings, is believed to commemorate the 1840 visit of Thomas Cole and William Cullen Bryant to Plattekill and Stony Cloves."

Another argument, put forward by Mabel Smith to claim the painting's locale for the Greene County site, was the fact that more than a century of weathering and vegetation growth may have somewhat altered the appearance of Church's Ledge in Kaaterskill Clove. Cole is known to have advised "to sketch from nature in the field and then, to select the elements which, when combined, make an artistic composition," and Durand and others followed Cole's suggestion. Hudson River landscapist Sanford Gifford produced an oil on canvas in 1880 entitled *Kauterskill Clove, Catskill Mountains*. In the left foreground is a plateau of rock, to the right is a steep sloping cliff, while a waterfall is seen in the distance. Gifford's composition is strikingly similar to that of Durand's *Kindred Spirits*.

The low-keyed controversy continues today. Mabel Smith wondered, "Was *Kindred Spirits* a Hudson River School of Art landscape made up of various elements to suit the ideals of Bryant and Cole?" In the final statement in her newspaper review of the controversy, Smith noted the overall importance of Kaaterskill Clove to American art history as "a tiny corridor of earth probably painted by more of the great and not-so-great artists of the nineteenth century than any other scene in their world."[2]

The United States Postal Service in 1999 produced stamps with the theme, "Four Centuries of American Art." One painting selected was Asher B. Durand's *Kindred Spirits*. The publicity for these historic stamps states that they portray "Thomas Cole and poet William Cullen Bryant in Kaaterskill Clove."

From the sketchbooks of B.B.G. Stone, 1854–1867.

POOR MAN'S ART

They occasionally turn up at auctions, galleries, or antique shops, and always attract the attention of potential buyers—lithographs of northern Catskill Mountains scenes of Kaaterskill Falls and the Catskill Mountain House. These lithographs were once sold for very low prices to hang on "cottage walls." It is said that such prints were the first exposure the lower economic classes had to the beauties of American scenery, and served to awaken their sensibilities to the natural environment.

The quality of the pre-Civil War prints varied to a great degree; some were the work of skilled engravers while others (like several of the Currier and Ives prints) were crude renditions varying greatly in quality.[1] The Currier and Ives print *The Catterskill Falls at Catskill Mountains* exaggerated the scenic view, but sold well. The undated print depicts an almost overwhelming force of water falling from the two levels. The composition shows the observation platform with its American flag, and two figures at the level midsection. *Scenery of the Catskills* is another undated Currier and Ives effort of uncertain date. Here a sedate hiking party is on North Mountain, with the Mountain House and the two lakes in view.

Benson Lossing's series that illustrated his 1866 publication *The Hudson: From the Wilderness to the Sea* were of finer line quality, but were still enhanced to impress the reader. Lossing's clove illustrations included *Entrance to the Katzbergs*,

Poor Man's Art

On Top of Haines' Falls, *engraving in A.E.P. Searing,* The Land of Rip Van Winkle, *1884. This view looks down through the clove to the Hudson River and New England in the far distance.*

Katers-kill Falls, Mountain House, from the Road, View from South Mountain, Scene on the Katers-kill, near Palenville (Moore's Bridge), and *The Fawn's Leap*.

After the close of the War of 1812, several English and Scottish firms saw a profitable market in illustrated travel books, portfolios of prints, and topographical views. European artists, either freelancing or under contract, found their way to the United States and were busy recording American scenery with pencils, watercolors or oils.

One of the earliest was William Guy Wall, who came to America in the year 1818. By 1820, Wall's artistic work, engraved by J.R. Smith and John Hill, became the basis for an expensive collection labeled *Hudson River Portfolio*.

William Henry Bartlett's topographical views, in both pencil and watercolor, found a ready market. Between 1836 and 1852 large quantities of Bartlett prints in medium and small sizes were produced, a number of which were used to illustrate N.P. Willis's *American Scenery*, published by a London firm in 1840. Among these was *The Cauterskill Falls*. One of his 1836 prints, *View from the Mountain House, Catskill*, was a best seller.

William J. Bennett's drawing of the Catskill Mountain House a few years after its first phase of construction was engraved in 1828 for the *New Mirror*. George Harvey's 1845 print of the Catskill Mountain House was engraved by J. Smillie. Catskill artist B.B.G. Stone produced several lithographs of note including views of the Catskill Mountain House, Leeds Bridge and Kaaterskill Falls.

The American Art Union produced a number of fine-quality engravings that were distributed to its members, thus acquainting many individuals of limited income with American art. The original artworks from which the engravings were reproduced were awarded to lucky ticket holders. Unfortunately, the American Art Union was dissolved as an illegal lottery.

As America prospered and traveling conditions improved after the Civil War, the touring public found the Catskill region to be a delightful summer experience. *Harper's Weekly* and *Harper's Monthly* were among the several magazines carrying artistic sketches to illustrate "description and travel" articles. Between the years 1866 and 1872, four individuals with superior sketching ability combined with a lighter touch of style came to the mountaintop to create artistic impressions for publications—Thomas Nast, Fritz Meyer, Harry Fenn, and Winslow Homer. They were among a new breed of artists who had produced field sketches during the Civil War. Thomas Nast became, in time, a political cartoonist of national stature while Winslow Homer brought the watercolor to new heights of excellence. His impressions in that genre gained him an international reputation.

Poor Man's Art

Composite views, some with humorous intent, were popular during the mid-nineteenth century. In 1866 Thomas Nast produced *The Catskill Mountain House*. The July 21, 1866, issue of *Harper's Weekly* provided its readers with the opportunity to be amused and entertained by Thomas Nast's *Sketches Among the Catskill Mountains*. The double-page engraving of twenty-eight

View from North Mountain. *North and South lakes, the Catskill Mountain House, and (barely visible left of center tree) Hotel Kaaterskill as viewed from North Mountain. This was a favorite sketching spot for artists in the 19th century. This image accompanied Lucy C. Lillie's article "The Catskills," in* Harper's New Monthly Magazine, *September 1883.*

The Clove in American Art

scenes and activities centered around Kaaterskill Clove. Nast combined humor with scenic appreciation. In addition to the predicaments of overly ambitious hikers and problems caused by excessively cumbersome steamer trunks, there are captioned views—"Haines Falls," Kaaterskill Falls," and "In the Woods."

For his *Catskill Mountain Album* (1869) Fritz Meyer created a series of individual scenes. Here we find cloves, waterfalls, the Mountain House—all above a marginal outline of the Catskill Mountains. These also were combined in a composite printing, sold separate from the individual views in the album itself.

If Meyer's album was for the masses, William Cullen Bryant's *Picturesque America*, published in two volumes, was for the upper class. Reviewers expressed their opinion that this was the ultimate in top-quality scenic sets. D. Appleton & Co. produced the American edition between 1872 and 1874. An English edition in four volumes (for easier handling) reached the market between 1894 and 1897.

Stereoview titled "Forest Scene, Catskill Mountains," by London Stereoscopic Company, ca. 1860-61. Note the artist sketching.

Harry Fenn produced the illustrations for the Catskill section. Three of his noteworthy sketches are *Sunset Rock*, *Catskill Falls*, and *Bridge in Catskill Clove*, produced in 1870.

Winslow Homer, following his Civil War experience sketching camp and battle scenes for *Harper's Weekly*, created *Under the Falls, Catskill Mountains* in which two young women steady themselves with long walking sticks as they watch a man and his female companion explore the concave section of upper Kaaterskill Falls. This image appeared in *Harper's Weekly* in 1872.

Today many of these book and magazine illustrations of the clove area have been separated from the texts and framed.

Enoch Wood and Sons of Staffordshire, England, produced pottery in a dark cobalt color, including various sizes of plates and bowls. Some of their products exported to the United States carried the underside identifications of "Pine Orchard House Catskill Mountains" and "Catskill Mountains—Hudson River." The Jackson pottery firm later on used mulberry and light pink colors in its "View of the Catskill Mountain House, N.Y."[2] Roland Van Zandt identifies this view as being from the engraving produced by Fenner, Sears & Company, which was based upon Thomas Cole's 1828 painting.[3]

Stereoview of footbridge over the Kaaterskill at Palenville. J. Loeffler, Catskill Mountain Scenery, fourth series, later 1800s.

From the sketchbooks of B.B.G. Stone, 1854–1867.

STEREOSCOPIC VIEWS

Few regions in the United States received more attention from commercial photographers in the latter half of the nineteenth century than Kaaterskill Clove. The grand hotels, Kaaterskill Falls, Haines Falls, plus the clove itself were all encompassed in sets of stereoscopic views. Today these are among the more sought-after paper collectibles.

In 1849 Sir David Brewster originated the portable stereoscope, based upon Charles Wheatstone's optical discovery written about in *Philosophical Transactions* in 1838. "By taking two photographs of the same object or scene from slightly different angles, when mounted side by side and viewed, one by each eye, the viewer sees a single picture with the appearance of depth or relief."[1]

From these pioneer efforts came the inexpensive, portable, handheld viewer to be found in most American parlors after the Civil War. Photographers and commercial firms found an almost insatiable demand for a wide variety of views, among these being the scenery of the northern Catskills.

Few early stereoscopic views have survived because they are especially fragile. One that did is Esther Haines Dunn's stereoscope, a pre-Civil War effort that depicts "Miss Patty Harbord, Abigail Dreer, Abbie M. Dreer, Mrs. Hill of Catskill, Mr. John Allen's dog, Fred J. Dreer and Fred J. Dreer Jr." in a group pose at the west entrance to the Catskill Mountain House. It is the amateur photographic work of S. Root of Catskill and dates from August 1854.[2]

Stereoscopic Views

Under a patent of November 19, 1850, F. Langenheim produced a glass commercial stereoview in 1856 of the "Catskill Mountain House from North Mountain." By 1858 his firm would be known as the American Stereoscopic Company-Langenheim, Loud & Company, Philadelphia. One of the firm's 1858 views is labeled "Kaaterskill Falls, Catskill Mountains, N.Y."

The London Stereoscopic Company, located at 54 Cheapside, decorated the reverse side of its "United States of America" series with an eagle and shield. Of the 150 or more stereoviews produced, one labeled "Forest Scene, Catskill Mountains" depicts an artist sketching by a lake. Tree stumps stand out in this view, and poetic verse is included to enhance the theme. Marked in pencil on this stereoscopic view is "circa 1860-61."

Winter in the Catskills: Sunset Rock overhanging Kaaterskill Clove, *stereoview by E. & H.T. Anthony, Artistic Series, 1870s.*

Bastion Falls at Horseshoe Curve, Rip Van Winkle Trail, *American Views* stereoview series.

By 1866, E. and H.T. Anthony & Company was a major seller of photographic supplies and equipment on both the wholesale and retail levels. For the price of a postage stamp, they would mail their catalogue to interested parties. The Anthony store, at first located at 501 Broadway, New York City, and later at 591 Broadway "opposite the Metropolitan Hotel," advertised a wide variety of paper wares, labeling itself the "Emporium of American Stereoscopic Views, Chromos, and Albums." Specifically mentioned are stereoviews of the Civil War, American and foreign cities, landscapes, and statuary. Also available were over 5,000 card photographs of higher-ranking military officers, artists, actors, statesmen, authors and prominent women.

E. and H.T. Anthony & Company believed in advertising. The prestigious magazine *Atlantic Monthly* carried their full-page ad on the back cover in January 1866. The first edition of Walton Van Loan's *Catskill Mountain Guide* in 1879 also included a full-page Anthony advertisement. In comparing the two advertisements, one notices increased publicity given in the latter to "A FULL ASSORTMENT OF STEREOSCOPIC VIEWS OF CATSKILL MOUNTAIN SCENERY." These views were not even mentioned in the 1866 advertisement.

A competitor in the production of Catskill Mountains stereoviews was J. Loeffler of Tompkinsville on Staten Island. Loeffler soon found that he had a profitable product in his first "Catskill Mountain Scenery," so much so that he produced at least four more sets under that same general heading. Both the Anthony firm and Loeffler assigned individual numbers to each stereoview. A label on the reverse side lists the views in that particular series. The numbers assigned were not always consecutive ones, the Anthony firm being prone to choose numbers in the 9,000s, while Loeffler preferred the 200s. Kaaterskill spelling was varied, with Loeffler preferring the valley spelling, "Cauterskill," and the Anthony firm "Kauterskill," while Langenheim used "Kaaterskill." To add variety the Anthony firm produced several series with special themes, such as "Winter in the Catskills" and "The Glens of the Catskill."

Minor competition came from A.J. Fisher of New York City, who brought out at least two series of "The American Scenery - Catskill Mountain Scenery." More locally, in Catskill the work of Allen's Photographic Gallery was limited to a few single views, including one of the Catskill Mountain House. Other stereoscopic firms included W.T. Towne (Lansingburgh, New York) and H.S. Field (New Hampton, New Hampshire).

The Bluff by Mountain House, stereoview by E. & H.T. Anthony, from their series The Glens of the Catskills, c. 1860s. This group photo on the world-famous escarpment depicts visitors to the Catskill Mountain House.

From the sketchbooks of B.B.G. Stone, 1854–1867.

E.T. Mason, Patron Saint of Kaaterskill Clove

To the early environmentalists of the nineteenth century, the commercialization of Kaaterskill Clove by the building of wooden platforms and stairways at the two main waterfalls—Kaaterskill and Haines—was not especially troublesome. Neither did the damming of the falls' water and its release for payment seem a travesty. But by the post-Civil War years, the painting of signs on rocks and the growth of "catchpenny" stands in the clove, such as one at Fawn's Leap, were a strong annoyance to many, including E.T. Mason.

The Mason family had made it a practice to summer in Palenville, at the foot of Kaaterskill Clove, to escape from the humidity of their Poughkeepsie residence.

E.T. Mason, Patron Saint of Kaaterskill Clove

Mason was then connected with a New York City publishing firm that provided him with a liberal income. After a time he and his family became more and more enamored of Palenville and the clove, and he began looking about for property that could serve as a summer residence. Brockett's in the Clove had been a convenient boardinghouse for artists such as Benjamin B.G. Stone, offering quick access to the

B.B.G. Stone (center) E.T. Mason (right) and Mason's son (left), photograph April 11, 1898. Stone and Mason were close friends and shared a mutual love of Kaaterskill Clove.

THE CLOVE IN AMERICAN ART

Fawn's Leap. *Photograph by J. Loeffler, Catskill Mountain Scenery series, 1870s. E.T. Mason purchased Fawn's Leap from the Brockett heirs and did much to preserve its scenic beauty.*

Brockett's in the Clove. *Stereoview by J. Loeffler, Catskill Mountain Scenery, first series. B.B.G. Stone purchased this stereoview May 5, 1876. Brockett's was a favorite stopover for artists sketching the clove. Accommodations were less expensive than those at Palenville or on the mountaintop, but were more primitive in the 1850s and 1860s.*

clove's more scenic domains at a lower cost than the Catskill Mountain House or Falk's in Palenville. When Brockett's in the Clove was put up for sale by heirs, Mason moved rapidly to purchase it. In the parcel of land purchased with the boardinghouse was about 400 acres of the clove, including the area surrounding Fawn's Leap.

The *Recorder*, a Catskill weekly newspaper, reported on July 23, 1875:

> Mr. Mason is a gentleman of fortune and a warm admirer of the scenery of the Catskill Mountains. He has purchased Bracketts well known tract of about 400 acres in the Clove, including Fawn's Leap. All the shanties and catchpenny contrivances are to be removed and the place restored to its original conditions and stonecutters are to be employed to remove the occasional business notices that have been daubed on the rocks.

The previous year the newspaper had praised Mason for his intention to restore that gem of nature, Fawn's Leap, to its original and proper setting.

Van Loan's *Catskill Mountain Guide* (1879) described the scenic sites in Kaaterskill Clove: "The road now curves to the left and takes you past the rustic cottage of E.T. Mason, to whom we are all indebted for removing the shanty at Fawn's Leap and with it the tax of twenty-five cents formerly charged each visitor at the beautiful falls." Van Loan's map shows the Mason cottage location.

The Masons were of the Anglican Communion and are credited with encouraging the formation of a summer parish at Palenville, served by St. Luke's of Catskill. Beers's *History of Greene County* (1884) states that Gloria Dei Episcopal Church was organized in the spring of 1878 with financial help coming from a "gentleman living in New York." It is believed Mason was "the gentleman" and that he contributed funding for the porch, roof, bell and windows of the church. Mrs. Mason is known to have raised money for the church's construction by holding a private fair at her Poughkeepsie home.

With their mutual admiration for the scenery of the clove, it is not surprising that Catskill artist B.B.G. Stone and E. T. Mason became close friends. Stone was frequently in the clove in clement weather sketching views, including one of Mason's Cliff to be published in Lionel DeLisser's *Picturesque Catskills, Greene County*.[1]

View in the Cauterskill Clove, near Mason's. *Photograph by J. Loeffler, Catskill Mountain Scenery, fourth series, 1880s.*

From the sketchbooks of B.B.G. Stone, 1854–1867.

B.B.G. STONE (1829-1906), SECOND GENERATION OF THE HUDSON RIVER SCHOOL

Benjamin Bellows Grant Stone, following a year's study at Boston and North Conway, New Hampshire, with Benjamin Champney, traveled from North Conway to view the Catskills for the first time in 1851. Next he studied one winter in New York under Hudson River School painter Jasper F. Cropsey. Stone again returned to sketch and paint the northern Catskills, and for a short time rented the "old Studio" of Thomas Cole, who was then deceased. Later, like Cole, Stone married a Catskill girl, Mary Allen DuBois and, except for the Civil War years, maintained a home in Catskill for the remainder of his life.[1] (A number of his pencil sketches and small oils have been on display in the Kaaterskill Clove Gallery at Thomas Cole's Cedar Grove.)

In July of 1881, Stone was sketching from his base at Palenville's Pine Grove boardinghouse. At that time he put down on paper his feelings about Kaaterskill Clove,[2] stressing that for half a century the clove had been a source of inspiration for artists and writers:

Benjamin B.G. Stone (1829-1906) painting in his Catskill Village studio in the later years of his life. There was a constant flow of visitors to the rented carriage barn off Orange Street (now Prospect Avenue).

THE CLOVE IN AMERICAN ART

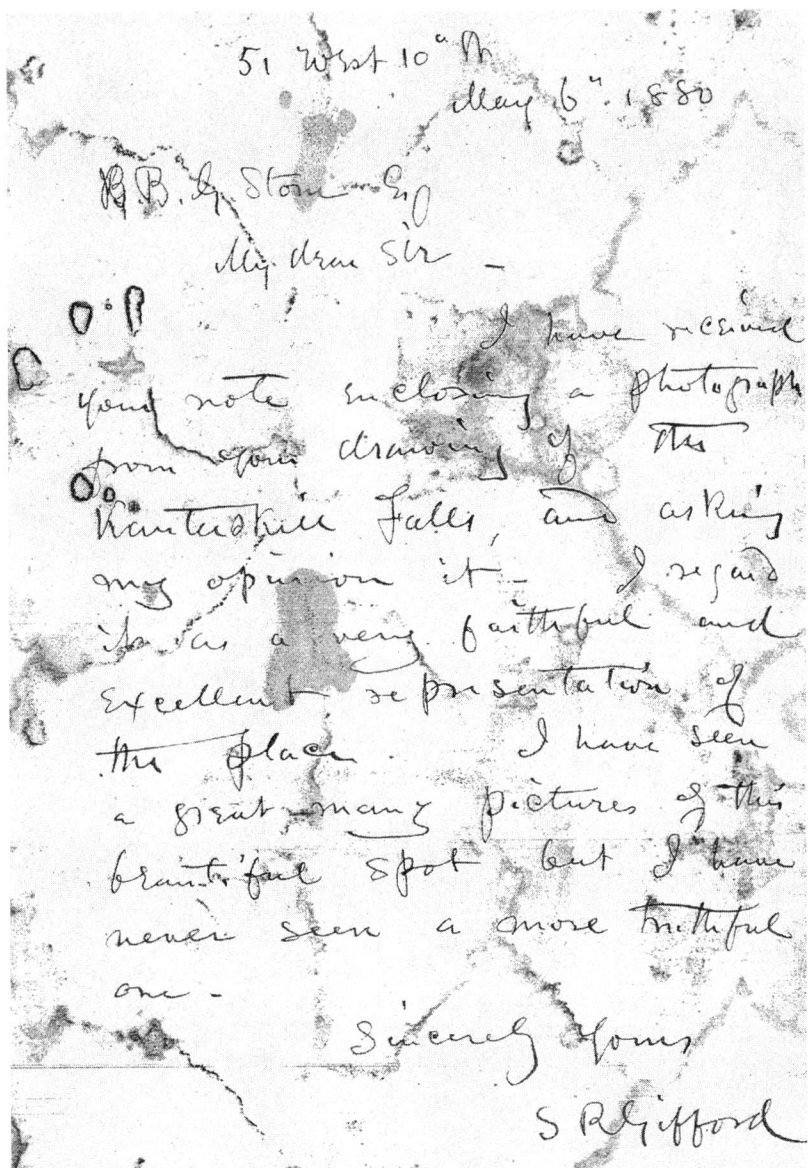

Artist Sanford R. Gifford (1823-1880) wrote to B.B.G. Stone from 51 West 10th Street, New York City, praising Stone's drawing, Catterskill Falls.

There is a wealth of beauty in this Clove to those who have eyes to see and hearts to feel, but it is no place for the frivolous and thoughtless. ... To see and know the Clove rightly is a work of time; hurried, careless visits give you no idea of its beauty or its grandeur and it has both. ... I have found a great pleasure in going directly to Church's Ledge in the morning or rather to the path which turns into the stream on the left, halfway between Fawn's Leap and the Ledge; the view looking down the stream is very fine there and will repay long and careful study.

Stone lamented that the upper section of the clove had been so vandalized by the tanning industry. It contained the grandest scenery of cliffs and waterfalls, but was spoiled by the bark peelers who felled hemlock trees, stripped them of their tannin-containing bark, and then left the stripped timber to rot on the hillsides.

Stone preferred the clove in August or September:

The chasm [is] a well-balanced picture, perfect in composition, color and light and shade. The background consists of the mountain sides south of the Clove, giving at this point a feeling of great height. The middle distance is composed of a strong mass of hemlocks, birches and pines in shadow, the tops only touched with light, the trees upon the hillside beyond this group being in full light, relieved by those exquisite purple shadows whose delicacy has passed to the utmost the skill of our best painters to respect. Through the center of the picture runs the creek with its never ending song of gladness; a pool of moderate depth surrounded by great boulders over which the water has poured for centuries, until they have polished and worn into fantastic shapes.

Twenty-eight years earlier, in 1853, Stone and a group of fellow artists had hiked and sketched in the clove. Young male artists at that time frequently traveled out of New York City and other cities to sketch in the country, sometimes with older artists such as Benjamin Champney and Asher Durand. Later in the summer Stone and his companions drifted about, sightseeing and sketching. By August of 1853 they were congregating at Palenville or at Brockett's in the Clove. A few sought lodging in the village of Catskill.

While some artists are better known today, few set down on paper a better expression of personal appreciation of Kaaterskill Clove than did Stone. His diary entries are most informative and bring the reader into the lives of younger artists seemingly always short of funds. The brief entries in B.B.G. Stone's diary for 1853 reflect his personal experiences as a young man attempting to earn a livelihood. His father never approved of his artistic career, even though his niece, Harriet Goodhue Hosmer, was a leading sculptor who studied in Rome and became one of the leading female artists of the mid-nineteenth century.

Following is a selection of Stone's entries for these three months in the clove:

August 14: Went with Casilear, Volmere, Johnson, Arnat & Lewis to see the Fawns' Leap—found one of the grandest mountain gorges ever behold—Arnat and I were left by the rest and lost our way—hard road to travel. In the afternoon layed off—had hard shower.

Monday at work under the Falls—made two sketches—broke umbrella a bit. [Note: The umbrella was a sketching device to shield Stone's head, face and hands from the sun's rays. The sketching umbrella is now in the Stone Collection of the Greene County Historical Society.]

Tuesday: Started in morn for Palenville to get stick mended—met Shepherd and Richards from Philadelphia coming up—stopped and began a rock near the bridge—In the PM I came down to Falk's—stayed all night—went to see some studies—very fine. [Note: Stone apparently stayed overnight at Connelly's and began to walk to Falk's boardinghouse to examine some artist's sketches.]

Wednesday: Rainy—Funny breakfast—hot corn, meat, preserves, pickles, custard pudding, coffee, bread & butter—went up the Clove with Richards & Shepherd and began to sketch—dinner same as breakfast only not as much fancy stuff—walked down the Clove in P.M.—found some good views—got some turpentine—bo't a cheap half. [Note: Apparently the unusual meals were at Falk's in Palenville.]

Sept. 6—Tuesday: Wrote to Sara, William and Stu, Harriet & Cropsey. Made five sketches—up at 5 1/2—bed at 9 1/2—Nat gone to Catskill—heavy shower in P.M. [Note: Stone corresponded with a number of relatives and friends. William may have been his older brother, Harriet his cousin the sculptor, while Cropsey was artist Jasper F. Cropsey. Stone had studied under Cropsey in New York.]

Sept. 7 Wednesday: Warm shower in P.M.—Made two sketches in color of leaves—Nat got home in eve—bro't papers.

Sept. 15th Thursday: Rainy. Streams very high—went to Palenville after a bottle of wine for Simpson. Bo't bottle of oil and lamp. Commenced sketch of Cascade back of tannery.

Sept. 16th Friday: Clear & cool. Nat & I walked to Catskill. I called on Mrs. Cole and was very politely entertained. I think the 2nd picture of the series "Cross & the World," one of the most beautiful pieces of landscape painting I ever saw. [Note: Thomas Cole's widow and family stayed on at Cedar Grove after Cole's death in 1848. Cole had been working on the series of *The Cross and the World* at the time of his death. The family would eventually sell the finished and unfinished paintings in 1873 to a Mr. Colyer, receiving $7,000.]

From Saturday, September 17 to Thursday, September 22, Stone sketched in the Palenville area, walked, and met with other artists. Some days he was prone to fits of discouragement, as on September 22.

Sept. 22nd Thursday: Tried to make a sketch & made a failure—I can't account for such fits at all. Went down to the Falls by the bridge, sat on a rock & studied running water. In evening read Ruskin & Cole. Everyday brings more proof of Ruskin's knowledge of nature. Autumn is coming and the season draws rapidly close.

Through most of October, Stone and his young friends stayed on, sketching in the open with the help of fires for warmth. On Tuesday, October 20, they went to Peter Schutt's Laurel House and the Catskill Mountain House. To their surprise they found the Catskill Mountain House closed and utterly deserted. Even the caretaker was not there. Stone sketched at North Lake and did sketches of North and South mountains.

Even with early snowstorms, Stone and Nat stayed on. The final diary entry before returning to New York City was on Tuesday, October 25.

Fawn's Leap from the top. Photograph by H.S. Field, New Hampton, NH, no. 19 in his Catskill Mountain stereoview series, late 1800s.

Buttermilk Falls in the upper clove. Photograph taken by L.W. Searing in July 1892, and presented to B.B.G. Stone on March 23, 1893.

October 25: Mostly clear. Hotchkiss, N & I went up to Schutts, then the Lakes and to the Mt. House. In going up we found the snow very deep and bushes loaded down with it and locked together—had a hard time getting through. The sun came out and the effect of its beams through the trees was very beautiful. Upon making the falls I was a bit disappointed in their appearance. It was snowing very fine. The rocks were all in a shadow except a passage on the left that was covered with snow and ice with long icicles hanging down from the crevices of the rocks. A tin that stood near the first stairway on the upper falls, was covered with ice and as the sun shown through it, it sparkled as if heavy with diamond. We arrived at Schutts and found no one. After waiting a spell we went on through the woods and across the fields to the lake. The snow was very deep on the way, averaging 18 inches in depth and a good part of the way it was two feet. We pushed into the woods on the edge of the lake and struggled through over logs and windfalls, sometimes rolling over in the snow and getting well powdered. The snow was very deep all the way through. After getting about half way we stopped to dine, scraping the snow from a big log and laying down a quantity of hemlock boughs for a seat. We sat down to dinner with an appetite sharpened by a hard tramp through the bracing air. After dinner we pushed on through wood and water to the Mt. House, and took our last look from the cliffs. To my surprise I found no snow in the valley, all perfectly clear. After trying for nearly an hour to get into the [Mountain] house we at last succeeded and were served by a giant negress, who heated up some coffee for us, while we warmed ourselves by the kitchen fire. We spent a couple of hours there. Saw Mr. Beach [portrait] and the picture by Bartlett (very bad). Leaving the house we started for home. The sky commenced clouding over and gave us some splendid effects. By the time we were halfway home there came on a severe snow squall right in our teeth. We reached home at last with wet feet and awful appetites. We were well repaid for our hard work in seeing the Lakes and Mountains in their winter garb, a sight that few are willing to take the trouble of seeing, but an artist should never be deterred by anything when in search of the picturesque. He should be willing to undergo fatigue and privation to secure his object, such men and such only are the true lovers of nature, who are determined to see in every season and under every aspect.

The next diary entry was entered in New York City, where Stone had set up in a studio at 359 Broadway: "I have at last set up my easel and commenced life as an artist on my own act. No one to depend on but my own observation and study."

That winter Stone worked assiduously with some success. On March 16, 1854, he finished his painting *Indian's Home* and sent it on to the National Academy of Design, where it was much liked. "I sent two others, 'Souvenir of the Catskills' and 'The Twilight Hour'," he wrote.

Stone's best effort was his *Catterskill Falls*, printed by John H. Bufford of Boston. Included on the engraving was the first verse of William Cullen Bryant's poem, "Catterskill Falls."

From the sketchbooks of B.B.G. Stone, 1854–1867.

THE PALENVILLE ART COLONY

In the late 1840s Asher B. Durand and his students came to Palenville, using it as a base from which to explore the clove to sketch and paint. Inexpensive room and board, important factors for young artists, could be found without trouble in Palenville. In the mid-1850s Benjamin Stone and his fellow artists used Brockett's in the Clove and Falks at Palenville for meals and lodging. Today, local residents follow Roland Van Zandt's and Alf Evers's lead and credit Palenville as being the site of the earliest American art colony.[1]

In the last quarter of the nineteenth century, the Hudson River School of Landscape Painting was in decline. Artists were more attracted to other spots along the eastern seaboard. George H. Hall, however, continued to maintain his interest in the Catskill Mountains, although he also had interests in portraiture. In his earlier years Hall had traveled about Europe, particularly Spain. In 1871 he purchased the old Palen store on the banks of Kaaterskill Creek near the westernmost bridge in Palenville. For years thereafter the building was a visual delight to passersby.

DeLisser's *Picturesque Catskills, Greene County* included a photograph of the attractive Hall studio with its fencing, flower garden and shrubbery.[2] Not shown are the large willows that the owner planted. The chimney, with its Spanish tiles that Hall brought back from Europe, was particularly entrancing to the passersby, especially amateur photographers.

The Palenville Art Colony

Palenville at the upper Kaaterskill Creek crossing near artist Hall's studio. Note the narrow clove road at the top right. Stereoview by J. Loeffler, Catskill Mountain Scenery, *first series, c. 1870s.*

THE CLOVE IN AMERICAN ART

The history of the building that housed the Hall studio was frequently imparted to visitors. In its earliest years it was a general trading store owned by the Palens, for whom the hamlet Palenville is named. The store was later kept by John Welch of Saugerties, who dealt in hardware. The next occupant was Elijah Trumpbour, who bought out Welch and kept a dry goods and grocery store until 1871. Hall saw possibilities in the site and persuaded Trumpbour to sell. Much of the ensuing architectural work was the inspiration of the new owner.

Walls, roof and floors were made double thick, with new boards placed over old. The hooded windows for protection from the summer sun were suggested from Hall's European travels. A balcony was more decorative than practical. The two large studio windows in the painting room, which was made out of rooms on two floors, were a necessity for the artist.

The studio room, as illustrated in DeLisser's volume, was filled with decorative acquisitions acquired abroad such as a Spanish monk's chest inset with pictures of hunting scenes, horses and carts, and gardens and fountains. Hall's collection of Oriental and Spanish brass and copper also gave atmosphere to the room, and there were oils on canvas painted by the artist. Hall was particularly proud of a painting from his earlier years, *Niobe Falls in the Clove*. Books, a Spanish sword, pottery and other items of personal interest filled the room with artistic clutter. Hall would summer in Palenville in his studio and dwelling until his death in 1913.

The relationship of Hall to Jennie Brownscombe has never been fully explored.

Palenville Overlook with the Hudson River in the distance. Stereoview by E. & H.T. Anthony, Glens of the Catskills series.

The Palenville Art Colony

Hall's studio at Kaaterskill Creek, Palenville, 1880s. Hall converted the studio from a country store. Tourists frequently took photos of the distinctive brick chimney.

Newspaper articles referred to her as "Hall's protégé." Brownscombe, a native of Honesdale, Pennsylvania, was a talented artist in her own right, painting local landscapes (especially with children), portraits of leading citizens, and historical themes such as *The First American Thanksgiving* for Pilgrim Hall in Plymouth, and *The Peace Ball* for a Newark museum. A number of these paintings are reminiscent of the type of duplicated sets of pictures once shown in grade-school rooms as part of art-class lessons.

After Hall's death his studio on the Kaaterskill, including the contents, became the property of Jennie Brownscombe. There she continued to paint in a style that some found decadent. She was an artist of national and international reputation in her time, and today there is a revival of interest in her works.

In late November 1921, the Hall-Brownscombe studio burned to the foundation with a complete loss of its contents other than a suit of armor, one brass utensil and the fire irons. The fire was a tragic loss to Jennie Brownscombe, but she soon purchased another building along the Kaaterskill in Palenville and returned summer after summer, while wintering in New York City. She made many Catskill Mountains friends and was described as enjoying good health, maintaining a sense of humor and having a keen interest in world affairs. At her passing she was the last artist of the Palenville art colony who was of professional stature.

From the sketchbooks of B.B.G. Stone, 1854–1867.

WALTON VAN LOAN, "MR. CATSKILL"

When the large volumes of the *New York State Biographical Review* were published in 1899 (alas, without a photograph of Walton Van Loan), the text included the statement that Van Loan was considered to be "the most reliable authority for the topography of the Catskills and no man in the county can approach him on the extent of information about this beautiful region. He has been to the top of nearly every peak." That same year it was estimated that some 36,000 copies of Van Loan's *Catskill Mountain Guide* and over 50,000 of his maps of the Catskills had been sold to date.

"A Fine Compliment to the Author of this Guide" appears in later editions of *Catskill Mountain Guide:*

> On leaving the famous Catskill Mountain House at the close of one of the four or five consecutive weeks after July 4th for our home at Catskill, we took the Ulster and Delaware train through Stony Clove for Phoenicia and thence to Kingston Point, on the Hudson River, to connect with the up Day Boat. On boarding the steamer, Commodore Van Santvoort, the President of the Day Line Company, who was on his way to Albany, stepped up to me and said, "How are the Catskill Mountains to-day, Mr. Van Loan?" I answered, "'Very, very fine. Full of well pleased tourists who admire the

> **Library of Congress,**
> No. 3877 G.   Copyright Office, Washington.
>
> To wit: **BE IT REMEMBERED,**
> That on the 31st day of March anno domini 1876 Walton Van Loan of Catskill, N.Y., has deposited in this Office the title of a Book the title or description of which is in the following words, to wit:
>
> Catskill Mountain Guide
> with Map;
> Showing where to walk and where to Ride
>
> the right whereof he claims as Proprietor in conformity with the laws of the United States respecting Copyrights.
>
> A.R. Spofford
> LIBRARIAN OF CONGRESS.

The original copyright document for Walton Van Loan's Catskill Mountain Guide. *First printed in 1876, Van Loan's Guide became an instant success and was reprinted for decades.*

world famed view of sixty miles of the Hudson River and the mountain ranges in Connecticut, New York, Massachusetts and Vermont." Mrs. Van Loan then stepped up and said, "Commodore, I should think you would be tired of hearing Mr. Van Loan talking so much about the Catskill Mountains." Commodore Van Santvoort replied, "Mrs. Van Loan, your husband has immortalized himself in connection with the Catskill Mountains." It was the greatest compliment I ever had. Then the Commodore invited us to take dinner with him on our sail to Catskill.

THE CLOVE IN AMERICAN ART

Van Loan (1834-1921), the Catskill Mountains guidebook author and mapmaker, was not, interestingly, a native of Greene County. He was born in New York City on January 8, 1834, the son of Matthew Dies and Julia Thomson Van Loan. His paternal grandfather, Isaac Van Loan, was a mason by trade in the village of Catskill, but for many years captained sloops out of the village's port on Catskill Creek. Isaac's small, yellow house was situated on Main Street in Catskill. Captain Isaac's wife was Jane Dies, named for her grandmother, the famed Mme. Jane Dies, who resided at one time in an imposing Georgian stone mansion (in later years referred to as "The Old Stone Jug") on the banks of Catskill Creek at the Landing.

Van Loan and his telescope frequently provided summer hotel guests with entertainment. Standing beside Van Loan are his wife, Lucy, and Sarah Beach, co-owner of the Catskill Mountain House.

Walton Van Loan, "Mr. Catskill"

The stately mansion was torn down during the building of the Shale Brick Works.

Walton's father, Matthew, was one of four siblings. Matthew left Catskill in 1841 to open a daguerreotype studio in New York City. He is credited with being the first man in the United States to make a business of producing portraits by this new process. Together with a colleague, Dr. Draper, Matthew successfully experimented to improve the photographic methods used by the French inventor Daguerre. Matthew Van Loan in later years was awarded many prizes in this country for his daguerreotypes and also earned special honors from England.

After a few years in New York City, Matthew Van Loan moved to Philadelphia and then to Washington, D.C. His wife Julia and their sons remained in Catskill; the marriage seems to have been a strained relationship, probably because of finances. Years later Walton spoke of helping to support the family by earning an occasional sixpence making wooden pegs at the planing mill next to old St. Luke's. Walton and his two brothers, Spencer and another (the latter dying young), were educated in Catskill. On hearing about the wreck of the steamboat *Swallow* on the rocks off Athens in 1845, Walton hiked the Albany and Greene Turnpike the following day to see the excitement. It became a good story, useful for entertaining summer resort visitors in later years.

At the age of twelve, Walton left Catskill to join up with his father, who was then in the nation's capital earning a livelihood as a photographer. Walton would occasionally help his father in the studio, where sitters included such noted national figures of the day as Dolly Madison, John C. Calhoun and Henry Clay.

> On coming home from school in Washington one Saturday, at noon, my father told me that on Monday I must go up to the Capitol, and in the House of Representatives, in the area back of the Speaker's seat, I would find eleven boys waiting for the Speaker to call the House to order; and then I must follow the boys to the cushioned seat provided for them in front of the House Clerk's desk, which was a long desk in front of and below the Speaker's chair. This was my first intimation of being appointed a Page.

This account, recorded in Walton's notebook, also became another story for hotel guests' entertainment in the Catskills, as was the great celebration and parade in Washington, D.C., for the laying of the cornerstone of the Washington Monument.[1]

When news of the gold rush reached Washington, D.C., Matthew Van Loan decided to embark for California, where he secured employment in the San Francisco Customs House. In 1852 Walton also gave in to the lure of California. Receiving a letter of recommendation from Daniel Webster, Walton set off on the shorter sailing route to California, which required an overland route via the isthmus of Panama. There is no record of Walton panning for gold in California. He worked first in the customs house, and then set himself up in a bookstore (or at least worked in one as a clerk). Walton remained in California until about the time of his father's death there in 1852.

Walton returned first to New York City and then moved back to Catskill, where he would remain a resident for the rest of his life and then be buried in Thompson Street Cemetery.

Having saved a little capital, Walton used the experience gained from his San Francisco bookstore venture to set up such an establishment on Catskill's Main Street. Walton also did photographic work at Van Loan's Ambrotype Room above the store. In 1879 Walton took into partnership his head clerk, Henry Van Gorden. Eventually, Van Gorden would buy the store, allowing Van Loan to concentrate on his guidebook and map business. The store still functions today as Van Gorden and Company. Walton's house on Prospect Avenue also still stands.

There were other efforts to earn income. During the locally famous trial of Joseph Waltz, for the murder of a scissor grinder and the subsequent murder of his Catskill jailer, Walton not only took notes, but also made sketches of the accused.[2] Walton's game, "Pendulum Oracle," which was "designed to answer any questions," dates from 1868. The game could be ordered at the price of one dollar. The "Magic Fair" game came next.

Walton married Lucy Baldwin Beach of the Catskill Mountain House Beach family in September 1874. Lucy apparently had a sense of humor; when staying with her relatives at their Mountain House before her marriage, she signed her name in the register and filled in her address as "Constantinople." Theirs was a childless marriage.

As the years passed, Walton and Lucy spent more and more of their summers in the northern Catskills. With his wide knowledge of the Catskills and his interest in astronomy, Walton and his telescope were always good for a guest lecture. Such efforts may have reduced their resort hotel bills. The local news-

Walton Van Loan, "Mr. Catskill"

Bear's Den, with its views of the Mountain House and the lakes, was a popular sketching site for artists in the 19th century.

papers, and occasionally a city one, would sometimes make good copy of Walton. Following is an excerpt from the *New York Sunday Tribune:*

> Walton Van Loan, the Catskill Guide and Mapmaker, who is sometimes greeted by his friends as a descendant of Rip Van Winkle, because of his intimate knowledge of the Catskills, has been giving much pleasure recently with his fine telescope at Santa Cruz Park conducted by Mrs. N.P. Leach, where he and Mrs. Van Loan have been stopping. On North Mountain he gave the fresh-air children of the City Mission in charge of Rev. and Mrs. Nelson a peep thru the big glass, to their wonder and delight. Expects to give new arrivals a view of the star [Venus] sometime next week by remaining over night at their mountain home.

On March 31, 1876, the copyright of Walton Van Loan's *Catskill Mountain Guide* was approved and issued by the Library

Hikers at Sunset Rock. Stereoview by E. & H.T. Anthony, American Views series.

of Congress. Selling at a modest price and including a map, the guide was reprinted year after year and updated as needed. In April 1876, Walton was granted a copyright for a "map of all points of interest within four miles of the Catskill Mountain House with roads and foot paths: Surveyed and drawn by Walton Van Loan."[23]

Would scenic views sell? Walton must have debated this question as the idea surfaced in his mind. Such a project called for skills that even this self-taught individual might have found to be a major challenge, yet he produced *Panoramic View From Slide Mountain—The Highest of the Catskills (4220 feet), Showing 67 Mountain Peaks*. Two sizes of this panoramic view were printed: one was 10 inches by 7 inches; the other was 5 feet by 14 inches. Both were lithographs in color and sold for fifty cents. *Catskill-On-The-Hudson, and Its Magnificent Mountains* was another effort. A third panoramic view, in color, of the Catskill Range as viewed from the Hudson River, sold for twenty-five cents.

With the coming of the Catskill Mountain Railway and the Otis Elevating Railway, Walton's map of Kaaterskill Clove was updated. It was a good purchase at ten cents, showing as it did the Catskill Mountain House, Hotel Kaaterskill, Laurel House, Sunset Park, Twilight Park, Santa Cruz Park, Kaaterskill Falls, Haines Falls and Palenville.

In 1884 Walton produced a decorative, hanging wall map, *Birds-Eye View of Mountain Resorts of New York State and How to Reach Them*. Included was the Adirondack region in addition to Walton's favored Catskills.

With the horse and carriage out and the gasoline-powered automobile in, Walton saw the need for a motoring map that could be included in his *Catskill Mountain Guide* or sold separately. The new map included all of Greene County, most of Ulster and Delaware counties, as well as sections of Albany, Schoharie, Otsego and Sullivan counties. It proved to be a popular map with many motorists.

Intrigued with a folklore story that one of his ancestors, Petrus Van Loan, had traveled down from the Saint Lawrence River to the upper waters of the Hudson River eleven years before the Hudson's discovery in 1609 by Hendrick Hudson, Walton produced a pamphlet via Dudley Press of New York City about the

Petrus legend. This was published at the time of the Hudson-Fulton Celebration (1609-1909) to claim some credit for his pioneer ancestor.

Lucy Beach was a self-effacing partner in the Van Loan marriage. She was born in Flint, Michigan, on October 15, 1842, the daughter of George Lewis Beach. In 1873, when thirty-one years old, Lucy came to Catskill for an extended visit with her Beach relatives. The proprietor of the Catskill Mountain House, Charles L. Beach, was her uncle. Later Lucy and her husband were frequent guests of the Mountain House when space permitted. One such sojourn was over the weekend of the Fourth of July in 1907. On hotel stationery Lucy wrote "chit chat" to her friend Mable in Catskill. The surviving letter reads:

> Fourth of July is over—there was a great crowd here, besides the guests of the house overnight there were 169 for dinner—we had to wait until the second table but everything was good—I don't mean us alone but all the family waited. It has been so cold I had to put on my winter flannels but today it is warmer. We are going to Minnie's Saturday as there is a large party of one hundred and fifty coming and all the rooms are taken.

After asking her friend to purchase a couple of linen collars, Lucy continued:

> I am feeling pretty good and eat well. Ida [Mrs. George H. Beach] sends a milk punch to my room for me every night and it helps to keep me warm—Now be sure to come to the Lodge and let us know what time and day you will be there. If you can not stay all night you had better take a morning train so as to have a nice long day—will meet you at the train.

Lucy died at the residence of Lewis A. Freese on lower Main Street in Catskill on March 29, 1928. She had outlived her husband Walton, who died on December 31, 1921. That she held him in deep affection is evidenced by the verse she selected for his funeral:

> Sleep on beloved, and take thy rest,
> Lay thy head on the Savior's breast.
> We love thee well, but He loves thee best.

Walton Van Loan, "Mr. Catskill"

The Mountain House lakes frequently were referred to in the 19th century as "Sylvan Lake." This early view contains the Native American legend of the spirit Manitou on the reverse.

B.B.G. Stone, Lower Falls of the Kauterskill, *pencil drawing, August 1853. During the 19th century, stairs existed on the left of Kaaterskill Falls and afforded tourists and artists access to a variety of views of the falls.*

III
LITERARY SKETCHES

The northern Catskills, and particularly the area around Kaaterskill Clove, held a special attraction for tourists for more than one hundred years. The famous scenery and hotels, local characters, and fellow traveling companions were woven into many travelogues and magazine articles. There was much duplication of content. The landing at Catskill Point, followed by a ride by stagecoach (or later the railroad ride to Mountain House Station), and finally the hazardous passage over the private toll road, were described again and again.

While the following is not a complete overview of the large number of accounts that found their way into print, it reflects the importance of the Kaaterskill Clove area to the traveling public.

From the sketchbooks of B.B.G. Stone, 1854–1867.

EUROPEAN TRAVEL WRITERS

There were a few refugees from the turmoil of the French Revolution who should not be overlooked, but by far the great majority of Europeans who crossed the Atlantic in the early days of the republic with the planned intent of writing descriptive books and articles about American topography and scenery were British. Some had special interests such as agriculture, botany, social conditions, and the relatively new political process. The Hudson River Valley gained much attention.

At times these authors made much of the rawness of Americans and their political, social and economic institutions. Welsh missionary Ebenezar Davis in 1849 wrote: "Our transatlantic friends are morbidly sensitive as to the strictures of strangers. They hate the whole tribe of Travelers and Tourists, Roamers and Ramblers, Peepers and Proclaimers." Earlier in the century came Henry Bradshaw Fearon's *Sketches of America* (1818) and Frances Trollope's *Domestic Manners of the Americans* (1823). Later on, noted English author Charles Dickens's *American Notes* was of a similar vein. James Fenimore Cooper was so angered at the negative views expressed in these books that he responded with a volume written anonymously. Had he published under his real name, it would have carried more weight, since he had an established international reputation for depicting American life and people. In *The Pioneers*, Cooper placed Leatherstocking (Natty Bumpo) on the Pine Orchard overlook, viewing the wide expanse and seeing "all creation."

European Travel Writers

The British professional travel writers have been the subject of much study in recent years.[1] Jane Mesick produced *The English Traveler 1785-1835*, while Max Berger's *The British Traveler in America 1836-1860* is equally informative. In 1982 Roger Haydon followed with *Upstate Travels—British Views of Nineteenth Century New York*.

Many but not all of the foreign writers managed to find the travel time to come up the Hudson River by steamboat, disembark at Catskill Landing, and take the stagecoach ride to the Catskill Mountain House with its famed view. Nearby Kaaterskill Falls was usually included in the journey. Kaaterskill Clove itself was treated lightly, if at all.

With the Catskill Mountain House in the background, hikers in the 1880s view the wide expanse of the Hudson Valley from the trail to North Mountain. Note the well-dressed men in their summer hats.

Literary Sketches

Looking down the Kauterskill from the New Laurel House. *This E. & H.T. Anthony stereoview was purchased by B.B.G. Stone on November 17, 1865. The reverse carries the Civil War Internal Revenue stamp.*

In 1876, the year of the Philadelphia centennial celebration, Charles L. Beach saw many of his yearly hotel guests opting for Philadelphia instead of the Pine Orchard. It is believed that the forty-nine-page booklet *The Scenery of the Catskill Mountains*, reprinted by the Catskill *Recorder* newspaper firm, was a Beach effort to offset travel to the centennial celebration. Among the fifteen excerpted literary efforts in the booklet were those of Harriet Martineau and British actor Tyrone Power. The inside front cover, title page, and the inside and outside of the back cover carry illustrations of the Beach hotel with promotional verbiage. One full-page illustration was the artistic work of E. Sears; the other was by Speer.

One of the most ambitious efforts to describe the United States in print was the three-volume set by James Silk Buckingham produced in 1844 and titled *America: Historical, Statistics and Descriptive*. Printed by Fisher and Son in London, the book was dedicated to His Royal Highness, Prince Albert. Buckingham had previously written about his extensive stay in India with side trips to the Mediterranean region and the Middle East. Buckingham brought his wife and son along for his American travels, and he gave a series of lectures to help finance travel costs.

In volume two we find the Buckingham family leaving Catskill on a Beach stagecoach in company with three other passengers. The trip to the Pine Orchard was described by Buckingham as "a tortuous route marked by deep ruts and large masses of rocks with constant elevations and depressions." There were many rivulets to cross with a minimum of bridges, and the trip to the foot of the Catskill Mountains took about two and a half hours. Nor was the stagecoach ride up the private road to the Mountain House any easier in the years before Charles L. Beach bought out the Catskill Mountain Association's interest in the turnpike. The association apparently had not maintained the toll road. The author gives much credit to the stagecoach driver and his use of a large, forked iron device to ensure the safety of the passengers when the coach halted to rest the horses. The device was designed to prevent the stagecoach from rolling backward down the steep slopes. Because of severe thunderstorms "experienced in all their fury," it took over two hours more to reach the Mountain House. The Buckinghams were soon fed and in bed.

The next day, a Sunday, proved to be almost a complete loss of time for the Buckinghams; the Mountain House was enveloped in a heavy fog most of the day. Up at daylight on Monday morning, the travelers were more fortunate and witnessed the rising sun. For all his complaints concerning the condition of the roads during the stagecoach trip, the Englishman had to admit it was worth the trouble, the effect of the rising sun being "most remarkable and totally different from anything I had ever witnessed." This from a man who had extensive intercontinental travel experience. That same Monday arrangements were made for a short wagon trip to Kaaterskill Falls. James experienced a sudden bout of illness, so Mrs. Buckingham became his substitute.

In a time when it was frowned upon for females to travel alone, Harriet Martineau was a woman of independence. With the profits from her writings, she would establish a residence at Ambleside in the Lake District of England, an area where such congenial individuals as Southey, Wordsworth, Ruskin, Felicia Hemans, Hartley Coleridge and Arnold Rugby also lived. Martineau also enjoyed the friendship of Charlotte Brontë. Volume one of her book *Retrospect of Western Travel* provides the reader with several favorable impressions of the Pine Orchard house and its scenic surroundings.

Tyrone Power, an ancestor of the twentieth-century stage and motion picture star of the same name, published *Impressions of America During 1833-35*. Included was his stagecoach trip and walk to the Mountain House where he stood "on the natural platform which thrust from the hillside forms a stand whence may be worshipped one of the most glorious prospects ever given by the creator to man's admiration." After seeing "the Katterskill Falls" Power vowed to return another time, a travel plan he was unable to fulfill.

From the sketchbooks of B.B.G. Stone, 1854–1867.

AMERICAN WRITERS— AMATEUR AND PROFESSIONAL

↠1825

Under the guise of "Letters to the Newspaper," an 1825 traveler's account of his side visit to the northern Catskills on his way to Saratoga appeared in the Rhode Island American with the headline, "Catskill Mountains. Extract of a letter from a gentleman to the friends of this town."[1] One can never be certain if such individuals were paid for their newspaper writings to offset travel expenses.

The 1825 account begins by mentioning that "I wrote you Monday morning from Catskill—that was an interesting day to me. After breakfast I went up the mountain in a coach, to the place called Pine Orchard." Later, joining with twenty ladies and gentlemen, they rode the short two-mile distance to Kaaterskill Falls in carriages and wagons, the latter made with four spring seats designed to offset the very rough road. After that they walked for some hundred rods to reach the small plank platform overlooking the falls.

Steps were not yet in place, so the gentlemen climbed down with the help of ladders to reach the solid rock overhang "serving as an umbrella." The writer noted the tendency of visitors to carve their names or initials on the rock. This group of visitors came in August and found the water flow to be low. Nothing was said to indicate any tourist shillings or quarters were paid to open a dam; however, a bottle of wine was sent down to some in the party by means of the pulley-and-basket arrangement. Following the Kaaterskill Falls jaunt, these hotel guests returned to the Catskill Mountain House for an afternoon tea, a promenade on the piazza, and finally, an evening musicale.

Artists' Rock was a popular hiking spot, especially with its shelter against sun and rain. This postcard was mailed August 5, 1908.

Literary Sketches

North Mountain hikers with the Mountain House in the background. The man carries a shotgun, the woman a hiking stick. This early view probably dates from the late 1860s.

They retired to their rooms at ten o'clock. The newspaper article's final line suggested that "Everyone who travels for pleasure and health ought to ascend the Catskill Mountains and descend the Catskill falls."

Written at the same time as Thomas Cole's first sketching trip to the northern Catskills, this 1825 letter to a newspaper may be the earliest of such accounts to cover a trip to the Pine Orchard.

1828

Books were popular gifts in the pre-Civil War era, and in 1828 the publishing firm of Carey, Lea & Carey of Philadelphia saw an opportunity to produce a travel book entitled *The Atlantic Souvenir Christmas and New Year's Offering* with that market in mind. The unidentified author included in this work "A Visit to the Catskills."

After quoting from Cooper's *The Pioneers*, the author leads the reader from the valley to the Pine Orchard House in a crowded stagecoach "drawn by four toiling horses." In answer to questions, the driver imparted information about Rip Van Winkle and "We stop at his shop—he keeps tobacco and drink and such like for travelers." From there the one male traveler decided to walk the remaining distance. Next came the tasks of securing accommodations and dinner.

The trip "to the Cascades" is described, involving passing a log cabin in a clearing. At the falls a small boy offered guide services "down the ravine," an offer which was accepted. That evening the rising moon attracted attention, as did the morning sunrise when the cloud of vapor melted away. Like many writers of his time, the author is endlessly wordy. The section includes one illustration—a full-length view of *Catskill Falls* drawn by Thomas Doughty and engraved by Geo. B. Ellis.

1840

A very interesting nineteenth-century American author who became increasingly popular with readers was Nathaniel P. Willis (1806-1867). In his day he was regarded as a well-accomplished poet and journalist especially noted for his travel books. He sought approval from the upper classes of American society and was seen as somewhat of a snob.

In 1840 George Virture of London produced a superior two-volume publication, *American Scenery; or Land, Lake and Rivers, Illustrations of Transatlantic Nature*. The volumes were well illustrated with the artwork of W.H. Bartlett engraved by the skilled hands of Coursen, Willmore, Brandard, Adland, Richardson and others. The text was provided by Nathaniel P. Willis who had enhanced his reputation with *Pencilling By the Way* and *Inklings of Adventure*.

The Five Cascades in the upper clove below Haines Falls, 1871.

Willis provided descriptive lines for the Kaaterskill Falls engraving and also gave an account of a harrowing sleigh ride in the Catskills based on another man's wintertime experience. A train of horses drawing a sleigh and passenger through deep snow in stormy weather became almost exhausted, but were revived when the driver provided them with some strong libation. The engraving was entitled *Winter Scene on the Catskills*. Such writing discouraged travelers from seeing the Catskills in the winter months.

1849

Families that subscribed to *Family Circle and Parlor Annual* were assured the contents of the magazine were suitable because the editor was assisted by an association of clergymen. The magazine had been established by the Reverend D. Newell in 1840, and by 1849 it was being carried on by Mrs. D. Newell of New York City. Surprisingly enough it listed a number of female contributors by name, both married and unmarried. This was unusual because at that time many women wrote under pseudonyms.

For the issue of September 1849, the view from the Catskill Mountain House's projecting rock platform was the subject of a short, anonymous introductory article. The writing had strong religious undertones that described "gazing down from an ethereal height on the world and its concerns." Also included were Kaaterskill Falls and South and North mountains. An engraving similar to others shows the view from North Mountain.

1852

Harper & Brothers established a favorable reputation among American readers by their careful selection of book manuscripts and magazine articles. Their *Harper's New Monthly* was subscribed to by the more affluent households. By the early 1850s the firm contracted with George William Curtis, author of travel books such as *Nile Notes and Howadji in Syria*, to write a new travel book. *Lotus-Eating: A Summer Book* appeared in print in 1852 and was illustrated by John F. Kensett. The volume sold so well that in 1854 a reprint was on the market.

"Catskill Falls," a chapter in the book, relates how the author and his two friends Olde and Swansdowne stayed at the Mountain House and visited the falls. While his two companions arose early to see the sunrise, the writer overslept and had to accept their description of "slanting light over a level floor of fleecy clouds, much more magnificent indeed, than any polar ocean could be."

The three men preferred walking to taking a coach, and they were soon strolling along past the lake guided by a finger-pointing sign that read "To the Falls." They came upon a very new and very neat white house "with a bar room."

Curtis introduces the proprietor as "the genius of the Falls" who carries on a trade in both spirits and water. Curtis then goes on to explain that Kaaterskill Falls' water can be "turned on to accommodate poets and parties of pleasure." The three paid to have the dam opened and climbed down the stairway. Soon coaches arrived with several females on board. Curtis does not neglect to mention the "friendly basket far overhanging the ravine upon an outstretched pole." After enjoying a full day at the falls, they decided to skip the Mountain House dinner and dine at a very small and clean new house nearby.

This Harper book is one of the better sources for a quality description of Kaaterskill Falls and its "living water."

⇒ 1854

In the pre-Civil War decade of the 1850s, Thomas Addison Richards (1820-1900) received a contract for a superior type of *Harper's* magazine article, with Richards providing some of his own sketches by way of illustration. *Harper's* was so pleased with Richards's effort that they made it the lead article for their issue of July 1854. Unlike many others, this artist-writer gave considerable space in his article to Kaaterskill Clove itself. He lamented the fact that of the thousands who visited the Mountain House annually, very few ever attempted to explore the clove proper, which Richards felt was of exceptional scenic beauty.

Richards was a member of the National Academy and is noted for his Hudson River School landscapes and portraits as well as his work as an illustrator and writer of travel articles for American magazines. An 1831 transplant from England, Richards grew up in Hudson, New York, and Georgia and became an extensive traveler.

Like many before him, Richards entered the Catskill Mountains region from Catskill Landing and was transported to the Catskill Mountain House by stagecoach. The first few days provided hikes to the two lakes, North and South mountains, and the falls, which Richards referred to as the Catskill Falls. Richards met up with the proprietor of the falls, Peter Schutt, "whom you must cultivate for selling off the water." The price for opening the dam's gate was "two and a half dimes the splash." Rigged baskets with bottles of champagne and other refreshments for the traveler could be lowered down from the small café, all to Schutt's profit.

The hamlet of Palenville was an economically poor village during Richards's visit. The industries that earlier had brought in settlers were on their way out, as steam power replaced waterpower and large, city firms competed for workers. Richards found Palenville "a struggling village," although he was able to find tolerable accommodations. The toll road was not for him; rather, he hiked along the Kaaterskill Creek bed itself—an arduous task. When he had completed the hike of

American Writers—Amateur and Professional

Kaaterskill Falls. Artist B.B.G. Stone acquired this E. & H.T. Anthony stereoview on July 28, 1875.

LITERARY SKETCHES

the lower clove, he emerged at "a rickety wooden bridge" (not yet referred to as Moore's Bridge). One day was spent sketching at the "Dog Hole," referring to Fawn's Leap.

Richards found East Hunter village in the clove to be a deserted area with a "falling tannery and sprawling shanties," the hemlock bark having been depleted. The upper clove's scenic beauty appealed to the artist in Richards, as it did to so many others: "Here is the favorite studio of the many artists, whom the summer months always bring to the Catskills." Every few feet Richards saw visual delights to be captured on his sketching pad—cascades, boulders, and finally "the Little Falls," as it had been so called in an earlier conversation with Peter Schutt (we know it as Haines Falls). Of interest is the fact that Richards bemoans the lack of nomenclature to suitably identify these various places of singular beauty. It would seem to verify the belief that such identifications as Church's Ledge, Moore's Bridge, Buttermilk Falls, Hillyer's Ravine and the Five Cascades were in general use at a later date, probably in the 1860s.

The Approach to the Mountains, via Catskill. *Artist's map of Catskill Point and the northern Catskill peaks, from the Hudson River Day Line guide book, 1894. The Catskill Mountain Railway transported passengers to Cairo, to the Otis Elevating Railway, or on to Palenville.*

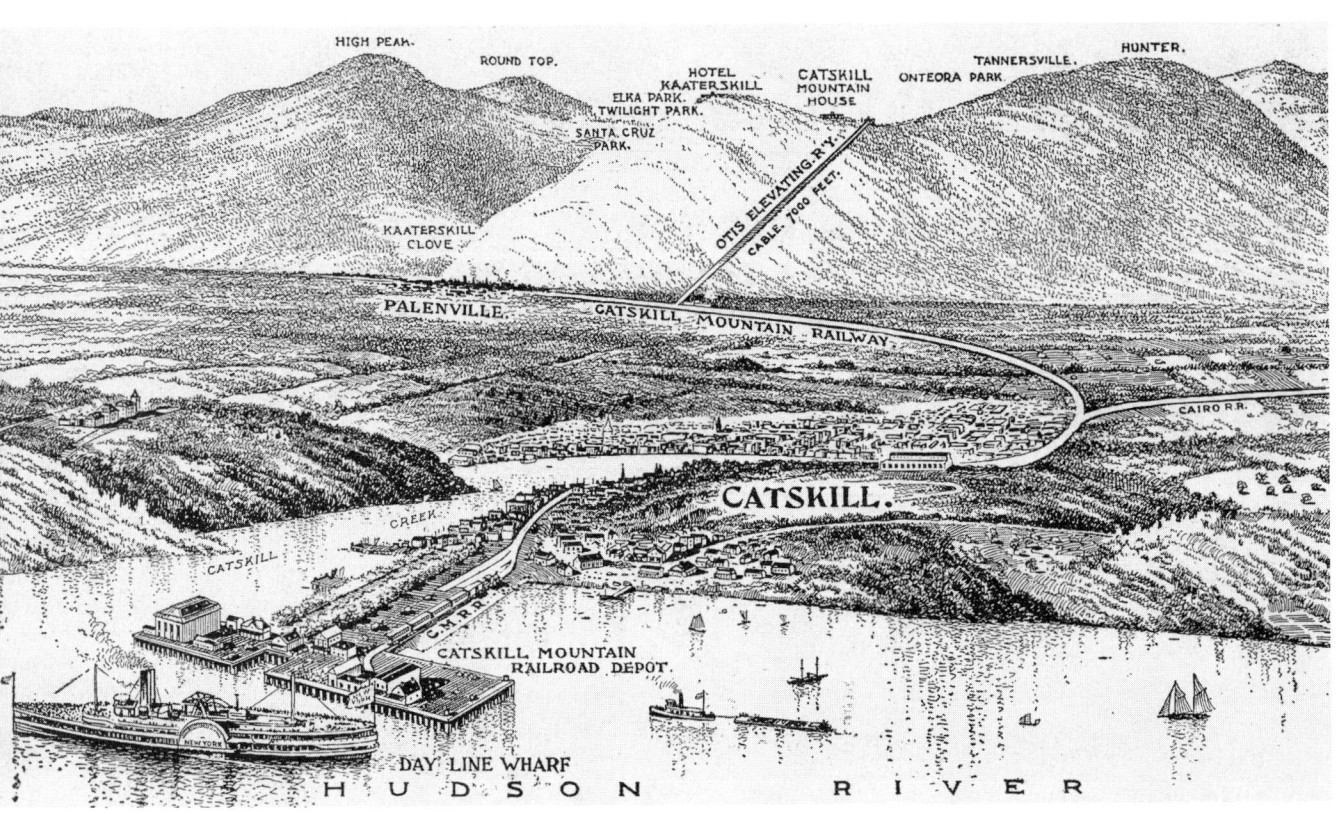

Stony Clove, Plauterkill Clove (Plattekill Clove), Round Top and High Peak were also part of Richards's magazine article, all based on firsthand hiking experience.

✒ 1867

The Reverend Charles Rockwell's publication carried the lengthy but informative title and subtitle of *The Catskill Legends, and History; with Sketches in Prose and Verse by Cooper, Irving, Bryant, Cole and others*. The revised edition came out in 1867, the first apparently a few years earlier. The book focuses the reader's attention on the northern Catskills, with mention of the Catskill Mountain House and other notable clove places.

Rockwell had been called to serve as pastor of the Dutch Reformed Church in Kiskatom, whose church and parsonage lay almost at the foot of the Mountain House overlook. Seeking out local history and legends among his older parishioners, Rockwell soon became a storehouse of local history in his own right. Prior to coming to Greene County, Rockwell had written *Foreign Travels and Life at Sea* based upon earlier experiences.

✒ 1875

Sunny Days on the Hudson: The Story of a Pleasure Tour from Sandy Hook to the Saranac Lakes, published by Nelson & Phillips in 1875, was written by Daniel Wise. Chapter 11, "Among the Katzkills," begins with the hiring of a private conveyance that permitted a more leisurely view of several scenic spots before ascending to the Mountain House via the Beach toll road. The writer makes much of the Rip Van Winkle tale and the haunting of the mountains by Hendrick Hudson and his crew. Two paragraphs cover Rip Van Winkle's cabin and the legendary hollow stone that still showed its use as a pillow for Rip's twenty-year sleep. Next comes a description of the landscape from the roadway, and finally the landscape as viewed from the Mountain House piazza. The next day the author goes to "Katers-kill" Falls. The season was dry, and the practice of releasing water to please the tourists is described. Unlike many other travel books of the time, this one includes a drive down the mountain to Palenville and up the clove to view Fawn's Leap.

The Wise book has 109 engravings, including *Entrance to the Katzbergs*, *Katers-Kill Falls*, *The Fawn Leap* and *Scene near Palenville* (probably intended to be Moore's Bridge).

✒ 1879

Lippincott's Magazine of Popular Literature and Science was a monthly publication aimed at a similar reading audience as *Harper's New Monthly*. In a two-part series (August and September of 1879) *Lippincott's* published "Catskill and the Catskill Region." No author is identified, but one suspects a Catskill village source. It is known that Catskill village artist Benjamin B.G. Stone supplied the drawings, or at least a major portion of them; the engraving was the work of H.M. Snyder.

The two-part article contains much local history and legendary lore passed down from earlier generations. The August issue explores "Old Catskill" (Leeds); the September issue covers the extended Catskill region. Residing in the wildest area is Diedrich Knickerbocker's evil spirit that brought about the birth of Kaaterskill Creek. The first illustration in the September issue is of Palenville, the entrance to the clove. Next comes Profile Rock, bearing the identification "on Church's Ledge." Moore's Bridge by Church's Ledge is still unnamed in that illustration. The reader is transported by means of side trails and the creek bed to the various scenic spots in the clove, including the base of Haines Falls. Many other sketches enhance the article.

⇒1883

Harper's New Monthly once again returned to Greene County with Lucy C. Lillie's article in September 1883. The author wrote of finding a faded letter of fifty years ago in which the letter writer spoke of a Hudson River voyage concluding with disembarking from a night boat at Catskill Landing. In 1883 the Catskill Mountain Railroad now ran to Lawrenceville, although the Mountain House station was still in construction. The agent sat outdoors selling tickets from a small pine table. As others before her, Lillie wrote of Indian lore and Manitou's great rock that served as his dwelling place.

⇒1887

Charles Dudley Warner's *Their Pilgrimage*, with illustrations by C.S. Reinhart, was copyrighted in 1886 by Harper & Brothers and made its way to booksellers' shelves in 1887. The artist and two male companions, King and Forbes, were on a summer's traveling expedition in the Northeast. King had visited the Mountain House a decade or two prior and was alert to changes.

Completing the narrow-gauge railroad trip from Catskill Landing to Mountain House Station, they were soon seated in a two-horse drawn wagon. Their traveling companions in the wagon were a man from a western state, his small and obnoxious son, and his two young nieces. Warner works in a good deal of humor in the narration. The boy was a constant critic of everything, including the Rip Van Winkle story. At the halfway point the attendant pointed out the surviving Rip Van Winkle artifacts and other items of ancient vintage, which finally interested the youth. The cabin used for selling beverages was described as built of "old boards brought down from the Mountain House some fifty years ago." The Mountain House itself, as King explained, was the center of attention a generation ago, and "going to the Catskills meant going there."

⇾1894

Appleton's General Guide to the United States and Canada, published in 1894 in two parts, provided the traveler with short descriptions of travel facilities available by rail and steamboat, and the more desirable hotels and resorts. The inside front cover of part 1 contains a full-page illustrated advertisement for the Catskill Mountain House. It was their seventy-second season and opening day was not until June 20. Perhaps to offset competition from Hotel Kaaterskill, the advertisement stressed that the Mountain House was the only hotel that commanded the famous Hudson Valley view north to the Adirondacks, east to the Green Mountains and the Berkshires, and south to the Highlands—an area of 12,000 square miles. The travel time from New York City was now down to three and one-half hours, and the Mountain House railroad station was only 300 feet from the hotel. The Mountain House Park, consisting of a valley frontage of over three miles and 2,780 acres, was promoted, as were the various drives to nearby scenic areas. The cooler temperatures, freedom from malaria, and other benefits were advertised, as were the "reduced rates" for 1894.

Appleton's guide contained three fine-print pages of textual information. In 1894 the Catskill Mountain Railroad was running six trains a day to Palenville, which included stops at Mountain House Station. The Otis Elevating Railway now provided the final transportation link of one and one-quarter miles to the Mountain House.

Hotel Kaaterskill and the Laurel House were included in the descriptive text, and it was noted that "At Palenville there are many boarding houses where artists most do congregate." Many of the scenic spots were covered: favorite places on North and South mountains, the two lakes, Kaaterskill Falls, Haines Falls, the rugged and picturesque Kaaterskill Clove, and Fawn's Leap.

B.B.G. Stone, pencil drawing of the lakes and the Mountain House. This scene from North Mountain was popular with 19th-century artists and was painted by Thomas Cole, Sanford Gifford, and Jasper Cropsey. The inscription "Met F.E. Church" indicates Stone encountered the artist Frederic Church along the trail.

⋇ IV ⋇
Grand Hotels and Private Parks

As agriculture and small industry declined in Greene County after the Civil War, the feeding and housing of "summer guests" in hotels or more modest boardinghouses took on increased economic importance for the region. The Catskills' distance from major cities was offset by improved steamboat and rail transportation. The two-week or longer summer vacation in the mountains became the norm for many city dwellers seeking an escape from the heat and humidity.[1]

Depending upon the degree of luxury desired and the amount of disposable income at hand, these summer guests had a wide array of options from which to choose. The rocking chairs on the piazzas were well used, but many found the time to walk or hike or hire a horse-drawn conveyance to explore the Catskill Mountains scenery.

Leasing a "cottage" in a private enclave wherein one owned the cottage but not the land was an attractive option for some families. Maintenance was provided and inns served the warm meal of the day, yet these cottagers had all the privacy and comforts of home.[2]

From the sketchbooks of B.B.G. Stone, 1854–1867.

SUMMER GUESTS AT THE MOUNTAIN HOUSE, 1880

Families who wanted reservations at the Catskill Mountain House in 1880 had a selection of seasonal rates to choose from. Between June 1 (opening day) and July 15, the thrifty could stay for a lower price: $2.50 for a day, or from $14.00 to $17.00 for a week. The same rates applied after September 1. During the height of the season, between July 15 and September 1, one could expect to pay more because of the higher demand: $3.00 for a day, and from $17.50 to $21.00 for a week. The rates depended upon the type of accommodations and the length of stay. Single persons occupying double rooms were charged extra. (Later in the 1880s the rates increased: daily room and board was $3.00 and $4.00; weekly rates to July 15 were $17.50, $21.00 and $25.00; weekly rates after July 15 were $21.00 and $25.00.) The hotel also offered seasonal rates.

Families with children and a servant could expect a larger bill at the end of their stay, but this could be reduced somewhat if the servant were housed in the attic chambers "under the roof."

Summer Guests at the Mountain House, 1880

Early tin plate image of the back of the Catskill Mountain House with a view of the west lawn. Photograph by S. Root, August 1854.

Glass plate stereoview of the Catskill Mountain House as seen from North Mountain, November 19, 1850.

Maintaining the distinction of class, servants were not permitted to use the public parlor and had to dine at the children's table. Children, with or without a nursemaid, were not permitted to romp in the hallways or public rooms. The rate for a child less than ten years of age who occupied a room with parents or with a maid was $12.00 for a week or $2.00 for a day.

Dogs were not permitted in any part of the hotel. Valet service was limited to the polishing of boots and shoes, for which guests were expected to pay the porter ten cents a pair.

Early risers could see the sunrise and cloud effects—the famous view from the hotel's veranda and one of the highlights of

Summer Guests at the Mountain House, 1880

Monday June 23rd 1856

Arrival	Names	Room	Residences	Departure
June 23	Geo. M. Eastup & wife	4	Brooklyn	B July 4
"	James C. Ward M.D. & wife		New York	B Aug 1st
"	Wm. R. Sherborn & Wife	11	Philada	B June 25
June 2?	Mr & Mrs L. ???	6	???	25 " 26
"	???	7	???	7 " 26
"	???			B June 25
"	???			B " 25
"	2 ???			B " 25
"	???			B " 25
"	F.E. Church	6	New York	B June 27
"	Theo. Winthrop	75	"	B June 27
"	C.H. Wheeler		Boston	" June 26
"	W.L. Whitmore		"	B " 26
"	F. Ingalls & wife		New York	B June 26
"	? Fowle	55	N York	B " 26
"	F. Marckwort		Washington	B June 28
"	W.S. Diggs & wife	62	New York	D June 25
"	D.P. Campau & wife	54	Detroit Mich	D " 25
25	Chas. Albertson	10	Philada	" " 27
"	S.H. Albertson	11	"	" " 27
"	Elizabeth B. Moon	11	"	B " 27
"	Colin M Ingersoll wife child & 2 servants	19, 18	New Haven	B June 27 / B June 27
"	W.P. Bleecker			" June 26
"	Mrs Bleecker	54, 4	N.Y.	" " 26
"	Miss Vidal	56		B " 26

June 1856 page from the Catskill Mountain House hotel register. Mr. F.E. (artist Frederic Edwin) Church and Theodore Winthrop of New York City arrived on Monday and remained until after breakfast on Friday, hiking and probably sketching.

GRAND HOTELS AND PRIVATE PARKS

The Fiero family of the Town of Catskill were among many who stayed overnight at the Mountain House in order to see the famed sunrise. Note the lines on the bill for extra charges such as a trip to "Katterskill Falls."

Catskill Mountain House proprietor Charles L. Beach studies the view from the escarpment, circa 1900.

Summer Guests at the Mountain House, 1880

a stay at the Catskill Mountain House—but they would not be served breakfast earlier than 7:00 AM. Nor could late sleepers order breakfast after 10:00 AM. The main meal of the day was dinner, which was served between the hours of 2:00 and 4:00 PM. Only children old enough to deport themselves properly were permitted to use the public tables in the dining room. Nurses and their charges were required to eat at the first serving. Instead of the customary supper, a tea was available from 7:00 to 9:00 PM.

Individuals visiting for the day could be accommodated with meals: breakfast was $1.00, dinner was $1.25, and supper was

Saloon of the Hudson River steamboat Daniel Drew, *c. 1870s. The steamboats transported visitors to and from the Catskills via Catskill Point. In good weather passengers favored sitting on the decks.*

Catskill Point was an important stop for Hudson River Day Line passenger steamers, especially on weekends. Photograph, c. 1880s.

$1.00. Should a day guest decide to stay overnight, lodging was $1.00 per person.

Guests who intended to use the hotel carriages or who wished to reserve seating on the stagecoaches serving the Mountain House were expected to notify the management before 10:00 PM the previous evening. They were warned that if they did not do so, they might find themselves stranded on the mountaintop, unable to meet train and boat schedules.

Regardless of their length of stay, guests were expected to sign the hotel register and indicate their place of residence. With couples it was customary for the man to sign and write after his name, "and lady." Room keys were to be left in the door slot or at the office before leaving the hotel. A safe was available for guests' valuables.

Activities, both indoor and outdoor, were numerous but weather-dependent. Carriage rides could be arranged around the Palenville-Kaaterskill Clove loop, and guests could take leisurely walks on easy grades around the lakes or hike the more difficult trails around the hotel. Boating and swimming in the lakes were popular activities.

The 1880 brochure, like others of a later date, stressed the hotel's healthy situation as one "free from malaria, chills and fevers, asthma and hay fever." Sufferers from feelings of debility would find increased vigor from the elevation and surrounding forests. The abundant water supply was "absolutely pure," piped from a spring two miles distant from the hotel, far out on North Mountain and surrounded entirely by spruce and hemlock forest.

From the sketchbooks of B.B.G. Stone, 1854–1867.

SUMMER GUESTS AT THE MOUNTAIN HOUSE, 1905

By 1905, the eighty-third season of the Catskill Mountain House, reservations were not accepted for any stay before June 26 (the new opening date). Travel time from New York City and its environs had been reduced from five to four hours, and travelers had a choice of means of travel. The Hudson River routes involved embarking from New York City on the steamboats *New York* or *Albany* of the Hudson River Day Line on any day except Sunday at either Debrosses Street Pier at 8:40 AM or from the Twenty-second Street Pier at 9:00 AM. The steamboats *Kaaterskill* and *Onteora* of the Catskill Evening Line left New York City daily, except Sunday, from Pier 43 at 6:00 PM. On Saturdays during July and August, the *Onteora* would leave New York City at 1:30 PM.

The Pennsylvania Railroad was available for those coming from Philadelphia or Washington, D.C., as well as from the intermediate stations along the way. Connections with the West Shore Railroad could be made at Jersey City. Once at Catskill Point, travelers took the Catskill Mountain Railroad to the Otis Elevating Railway, which took them to Otis Summit, only 300 feet from the hotel.

Other routes were available. "Those preferring to come via Rhinebeck, Rondout or Kingston might use the New York Central and Hudson River Railroad to

Summer Guests at the Mountain House, 1905

The Otis Elevating Railway was the final link between Catskill Point and several Town of Hunter connections. The Otis eliminated the difficult horse-and-carriage trip over the private Beach toll road. Photograph by J. Loeffler, 1892.

Ledge of Rocks in front of Mountain House. *Photograph by J. Loeffler, 1892. Note the absence of iron fencing, an addition that would be made later for safety.*

Rhinebeck; Hudson River Day Line to Kingston Point; Rondout Night Line to Rondout; West Shore Railroad to Kingston; Ulster and Delaware to Kaaterskill station which was three-quarters of a mile from the Hotel. [By this time the Ulster and Delaware was operating the Stony Clove and the Kaaterskill lines.]" Stages were available to transport individuals and their luggage.

Once the method of travel was decided upon, travelers were urged to purchase "through" tickets and have their baggage checked to either Otis Summit or Kaaterskill Station.

A pictorial promotion booklet was published by the *Recorder* press in Catskill. The booklet stressed that the Catskill Mountain House was "the only hotel that commands the Famous View of the Hudson Valley," as it was situated on the "Front of the Range." The booklet stated that the famous view encompassed 12,000 square miles, including 60 miles of the Hudson River. "The Mountain House Park consists of 2780 acres of forest and farm lands, traversed in all directions by miles of wood trails and carriage roads. The grandest views are to be obtained from the North Mountains—The Crest, Newman's Ledge, Bear's Den

The July 4, 1892, Van Gelder-Wardle picnic expedition via the Otis Elevating Railway. J.H. Van Gelder of Catskill gave illustrated lecture tours around the United States to cover the cost of family travels. Note the curtains on the cable cars for inclement weather.

GRAND HOTELS AND PRIVATE PARKS

and Prospect Rock. On South Mountain are Eagle Rock and Palenville Overlook. Both North and South Lake are within the hotel's boundaries."

For the 1905 season the Beach family had invested money to modernize the hotel's kitchen and dining room, which could now accommodate two seatings for an additional 150 guests. Tables were well supplied with fresh vegetables and eggs from farms at the base of the mountain. The hotel farm with its herd of Alderney cows provided fresh milk and cream. Fresh fish, poultry, game and meats were brought in at an early hour each morning from New York City suppliers and stored in coolers using ice harvested in the winter from South Lake. A French chef was in charge of the kitchen.

Entertainment was readily available both day and night. Outdoor amusements included boating on the lakes, managed by Messrs. Byliss and Hoff, from Bayonne, New Jersey. They offered canoes, outriggers and rowboats for rental. A number of new trails

The village of Haines Falls, where the competing Ulster-Delaware and Stony Clove Railroad and the Catskill and Tannersville line had their own stations. Local hotels and boardinghouses met guests at the stations and provided transportation to their establishments. This postcard is dated August 18, 1906.

Summer Guests at the Mountain House, 1905

The Bluff by Mountain House, 1870s. *Stereoview by E. & H.T. Anthony, Glens of the Catskills series.*

Power house, Otis Elevating Railway, 1890s. Photograph by J.H. Van Gelder for his illustrated lectures.

Otis Elevating Railway in operation. Photograph by J. Loeffler, 1892. Note the station building at the foot of the incline.

had been created for walkers and hikers wishing to enjoy the pure mountain air. The livery could furnish comfortable surreys and mountain traps (light, two-wheeled carriages) for large parties.

Tennis, croquet and quoits (a game similar to horseshoes) could be played on the west lawn while observing spectators sat on the west piazza. Baseball had come into its own as a very popular sport. The Mountain House fielded a team comprised of staff and volunteers from the guest list that played both practice and match games. A popular evening entertainment was watching from the front piazza as the powerful searchlight placed on the east front shone its light from 9:00 to 11:00 PM on the 12,000-square-mile, five-state view.

For the less physically active guests, whist and euchre card parties could be arranged. The hotel's orchestra rendered a morning concert every weekday, and played dance music in the evenings.

Kaaterskill Falls was still identified as Cauterskill Falls in the 1905 booklet. The boathouse on South Lake was a featured illustration with its busy boats. A full-page view of the hotel in 1830 stressed the age and history of the establishment.

This booklet, unlike others in subsequent years, was dated and thus had to be updated in later years as prices changed. Such promotional paper items, in addition to providing a better understanding of the famed hotel's operation, are also very collectible today.

An Otis Elevating Railway cable car ascending the mountain. Photograph by J. Loeffler, 1892. Passengers are riding backward so as to enjoy the view. Note the conductor by the safety wheel.

From the sketchbooks of B.B.G. Stone, 1854–1867.

HOTEL KAATERSKILL

It has been said that George W. Harding of Philadelphia was so enamored with the name "Kaaterskill" that he used it wherever he could. On the front cover of his hotel's promotional booklet, "Kaaterskill" appears eight times. He even rechristened South Mountain and South Lake as Kaaterskill Mountain and Kaaterskill Lake.

The drawing in the 1892 booklet produced by Levy Type Company of Philadelphia remains striking, even though it exhibits some artistic license and promotional distortion. Crowning the highest section of South Mountain, Hotel Kaaterskill's view must have been almost as impressive as that of its aging rival, the Catskill Mountain House. Especially noticeable in this artistic sketch are the prominence of the Otis Elevating Railway and the complete absence of the landmark Catskill Mountain House.

In recent years much has been made of the Hotel Kaaterskill-Catskill Mountain House rivalry. The outburst of temper from George W. Harding over the inability of his family to secure a chicken dish not on that day's menu at the Catskill Mountain House, however, is somewhat of an exaggeration. Accounts of the episode vary. One account blames the Beach management for their unwillingness to serve chicken broth at breakfast for an ill member of the Harding family, while others credit "fried chicken" as the culprit, resulting in Harding declaring that he would build his own hotel.

Hotel Kaaterskill

The private road up South Mountain from Palenville to the Hotel Kaaterskill. Round Top looms in the distance.

The *Catskill Evening Mail* issue of November 29, 1880, contains an article on the building of the new Harding Hotel that states that Harding "for the past several years had been seriously contemplating the building of a very modern hotel and had been studying various sites' potential, finally settling on South Mountain. The Hotel is to be called South Mountain Hotel, the acreage including scenic Sunset Rock."

Once he had definitely made up his mind, wealthy patent lawyer Harding moved rapidly to have his summer resort hotel open for the 1881 season. S.D. Button, employed as the architect, was from Philadelphia as was the plumbing contractor. As the site construction got underway, a top priority was the construction of a direct access roadway up South Mountain from the Kaaterskill Clove entrance area. Confounding the naysayers, the Edward Dibble and Collins Hyser crew were successful in building this road over difficult terrain. Harding also planned a private driving and walking park on South Mountain.

The construction of this large hotel made good newspaper copy, and the local weeklies made much of it. Rumors circulated concerning the payment of the workmen with specie (coin) brought in by kegs, and the waste of money by over-ordering supplies of lath and other building materials (which were simply hidden in the walls so the waste wouldn't be discovered). There was also the rumor of Harding's effort to rename South Mountain as Kaaterskill Mountain.

Edward A. Gillett of the Colonade Hotel in Philadelphia was hired to manage Hotel Kaaterskill. He began taking reservations for the summer of 1881 from a New York City location, and the hotel opened in July 1881 as promised, although work continued for another two years.

In the "Summer Resort" section of the *New York World* and elsewhere, Gillett sought to secure the patronage of a higher-class clientele. The advertisement of July 7, 1882, from the Mabel Parker Smith Collection reads: "HOTEL KAATERSKILL NOW OPEN: LARGEST MOUNTAIN HOTEL IN THE WORLD. Fifteen degrees cooler than New York City. Railroad communications now completed within one hour's ride of the hotel." The advertisement offered the public a choice of routes from New York City. Taking the New York Central and Hudson River Railroad via Rhinebeck, one could arrive at Hotel Kaaterskill in six hours. A second route was via Rondout, using Hudson River Day Line steamboats leaving New York City from the Harrison Street terminal. Guests were instructed to purchase tickets and check baggage to Tannersville Junction via the Ulster and Delaware and Stony Clove Railroad. No mention was made of the stagecoach route from Catskill Point, but in a July 26 news item for metropolitan readers that same year, the Catskill route was mentioned. That news clipping, also from the Mabel Parker Smith Collection, is worth quoting in its entirety.

A Pleasant Summer Hotel
The Hotel Kaaterskill, situated in the Catskill Mountains may now be reached from two directions—from Catskill village on the Hudson by an agreeable carriage drive of about twelve miles, and from Tannersville on the new Stony Clove Railroad, which, branching off from the Ulster and Delaware Railroad, runs along the western slope of the mountain range upon which

Hotel Kaaterskill

the hotel stands. The distance from Tannersville by the Hotel stage is but an hour's drive through a picturesque country. The hotel this year has become a post station and is called the Kaaterskill Post-Office, Greene County, N.Y. A few changes in the interior of the house have been made and the parlors are now on the ground floors, in proximity to the rotunda and the porticoes, which have been extended around the house. A miniature lake of spring water has been constructed on the grounds, and a path has been made to South Lake, where boats for rowing and fishing are provided. Many new drives have been made, the most important of which follows the crest of the mountain to the Point of Rocks, where a handsome casino will be built. The comforts and conveniences of the hotel consist of steam elevators, electric bells, steam heating apparatus, open-grate fires, gas throughout, bath-rooms and suites of rooms with private baths and closet toilets. The Germania orchestra, of Philadelphia, gives concerts night and morning.

The Hotel Kaaterskill brochure of 1891, aimed at "Heads of Families," called attention to the hygienic features of this summer resort. While the elevation had

Hotel Kaaterskill, c. 1881. The large annex has not yet been built.

Main dining room of the Hotel Kaaterskill, 1880s. Note the size of the all-male wait staff, the gas lighting, and the water bottles on each table.

shrunk mysteriously from the 3,000 feet alleged in earlier publicity to "about 2800 feet," the moderate temperature, "seldom above seventy-five degrees," was stressed as was the absence of flies and mosquitoes. Its pure and abundant drinking water was praised by Professor Leeds of the Stevens Institute and Professor W. P. Mason of Rensselaer Polytechnic Institute. All hotel sanitary conveniences and waste drainage was under the supervision of a sanitary engineer. A resident physician's services and a well-stocked pharmacy were added promotional points.

Food received special mention, with milk and cream coming twice daily from the Kaaterskill dairy, which adhered to exceptional standards. Vegetables were from the Kaaterskill farm, and meats from the Kaaterskill abattoir. With fire in wooden structures always a concern, parents were reassured that fire wardens were assigned to night patrol duty in the hallways.

The Hotel Kaaterskill, like the Catskill Mountain House, had its own in-house printing staff to meet such needs as printing daily menus. The first year's menus, on cream-colored stock, depicted a frontal view of the four-story structure with its tower-

Boulder Rock on South Mountain. Stereoview by E. & H.T. Anthony, acquired by B.B.G. Stone on July 28, 1875. Note graffiti on the rock.

like appendages. On the reverse side of the menu was an advertisement from the noted Philadelphia jewelry firm of Bailey, Banks and Biddle focusing the reader's attention on the availability of "Fine Diamonds—Solitaires and Matched Pairs; Rare Gems, Sapphires, Rubies, Pearls." This advertisement is an indication of the importance of guests from Philadelphia at the Hotel Kaaterskill.

A Sunday dinner menu for August 7, 1881, survives. Edward Gillet is credited as the manager, but Harding is not mentioned. In addition to soup and fish courses, meat and vegetable choices were many. For those preferring a cold Sunday dinner in hot August, chicken salad, boned turkey, smoked tongue and pickled salmon were offered. Desserts included pastries, fruits, ice cream, puddings and wine jelly. The Sunday dinner table included an assortment of cheeses, nuts and raisins. But alas, there was no fried chicken!

The menu offered a substantial wine and beverage list with champagne, claret, burgundy, sauterne, port, Madeira and sherry (both domestic and foreign), hock, whiskies, ale, porter and cor-

A carriage at the main entrance to Hotel Kaaterskill. The annex has now been added to the hotel complex.

dials. Prices were by pint or quart (except for ale, porter and cordials), and ranged from $4.00 down. For those preferring nonalcoholic drinks, mineral waters could be ordered, including Congress Water from Saratoga Springs.

Harding's vision of a profitable summer hotel on South Mountain proved to be a realistic one, so much so that in a few years' time he was contracting for a large four-story annex connected to the main building by a sheltered walkway. If there were any doubts that his establishment was the largest mountain house in the world, the annex would substantiate his publicity claims. For the summer of 1884, manager W.F. Paige had 148 additional rooms for guests plus a new opera house. While Harding could see little or no financial profit in keeping the main hotel open for the month of September, he was willing to accommodate hay fever sufferers in the annex. To that purpose, separate cooking and dining facilities were installed in 1885 so that the annex could operate on its own after the main building closed by Labor Day weekend.

There was nothing second-class about the annex. It had handsome, cherry wood furniture, Brussels carpet, baths, and ample closet space. The second-floor suite of nine rooms located at the southeast corner with its superb view of the Hudson Valley was designated for the anticipated stay of President Ulysses S. Grant and party in August 1885.

Continued improvements were always being carried out, such as the extension of the electric bells, which could now summon service to all bedrooms. And how many summer resorts could boast of their own opera house now providing concerts, balls, and amateur theatricals? "Yes," a reporter wrote, "annex and hotel combined will accommodate a regiment of persons and two companies."

The New York Times in early July issues of both 1885 and 1886 provided its readers with a foretaste of summer delights away from the heat of the cities. Both articles give first-place coverage to Hotel Kaaterskill, followed by the Catskill Mountain House, and finally the Laurel House—the three summer hotels along the eastern range of the Catskill Mountains. South Mountain was now referred to as Kaaterskill Mountain, reflecting the wishes of Harding. Travel time from metropolitan New York City and elsewhere was cut substantially with the building of the Kaaterskill Railroad and the Otis Elevating Railway.

The growth of the prohibition movement in the town of Hunter in 1891 was of serious concern to Harding, especially when three excise commissioners pledged to "no license" the town. Harding quickly invited a number of state legislators, to be wined and dined and to discuss the movement of Hotel Kaaterskill land and buildings boundaries into the town of Catskill, if Hunter were to go dry. With his powerful contacts and threats on the local level, the temperance issue was buried.

Over the winter of 1905-1906, $20,000 was expended on improvements for the convenience of Hotel Kaaterskill guests. Advertising in the *New York Herald* that season, the hotel's management proclaimed: "Through Pullman Car Service, Clientele the most Exclusive, Cuisine and Service Unequalled, and Magnificent Park." Entertainment was varied and included golf, tennis, bowling, fishing, boating and canoeing for the more active, while the livery stable provided horse and carriage trips for more leisurely outdoor enjoyment. The more sophisticated could also while away the evening hours in the German rathskeller.

Unlike the Beach family, which held an elaborate Catskill Mountain House reception for Mary Beach's marriage to John K. Van Wagonen in 1911, the earlier wedding of Anne Bigelow, daughter of John Bigelow (ex-secretary of state of New York), to Butler Harding (son of George Harding) was held in Ulster County. The reception was held at The Squirrels (the summer home of the Bigelow family). The groom had his brother, George Harding Jr., serve as best man. Bishop Davies of Philadelphia performed the ceremony. Over 250 friends and relatives were present.

The changing times affected Hotel Kaaterskill. As early as the season of 1889, W. F. Gilsey was not taking reservations until June 15, and reduced rates of $21.00 a week were available except for the peak months of July and August.

After the opening of the rail connections from Catskill, many local cyclists made use of the Hotel Kaaterskill Park, but to their dismay they soon faced a charge of twenty cents per wheel.

The Hotel Kaaterskill remained in the Harding family for a time after the death of George Harding in New York City on November 17, 1902. Butler Harding had died before his father, and there is no indication he ever helped manage Hotel Kaaterskill. The two remaining heirs were George's son, George Jr., and a daughter, Eliza. The George Harding Jr. family is known to have been at the hotel overseeing the family property, for it was there that their eighteen-month-old daughter, Madeline, died.

At times George Jr. even debated the advisability of opening for the season, as in the year 1911. Driving up from Philadelphia in his new automobile, he arranged for the sale of most of the hotel's livery horses. At that time he also offered to lease the hotel to Louis Frankel Jr. The latter agreed and immediately went to Albany to incorporate the Frankel Hotel Company with $10,000 in capital stock. Finally, in 1921, a buyer was found in Harry Tannenbaum of Lakewood, New Jersey. Tannenbaum purchased the Hotel Kaaterskill property for $125,000 using the corporate name of the St. Regis Restaurant Company of New York. Under Tannenbaum's direction the hotel was revitalized for a few seasons until, on the evening of September 8, 1924, it burned in a spectacular fire said to be accidentally caused while some employees were rendering fat for soap.

The Tannenbaums were soon busy proposing to build a cottage park near the clove overlook. A clubhouse would have a central dining area. The hotel buildings that were not consumed by the fire would have utilitarian uses. But this concept of seasonal cottages was never developed. Tannenbaum's death without a will left as administratrix Millie Tannenbaum. Claims against the property called for legal action on the part of creditors such as the Upper Hudson Electric and Railroad Company for services to Hotel Kaaterskill.

The final chapter came on June 6, 1930, when the State of New York purchased the land to add it to the state park, paying the Depression-era low price of $6,196.00 for the 619.6 acres.

The increased popularity of the North-South Lake State Park encouraged the state to purchase additional acreage for hiking trails and scenic protection. On March 3, 1933, the state bought a tract of 252.6 acres east of and adjoining the former Tannenbaum holdings, paying $10 per acre. The park increased further when Columbia University sold its 57-acre parcel just south of the Catskill Mountain House site for $31,500.

Otis Summit. Terminus of the Otis Elevating Ry. and the Kaaterskill R.R. *Composite drawing from an 1899 brochure for the Hudson River Day Line, showing the Otis Elevating power house and towered cable wheel in relative location to the Catskill Mountain House and Hotel Kaaterskill. Note the three passenger cars that are parked by the power house.*

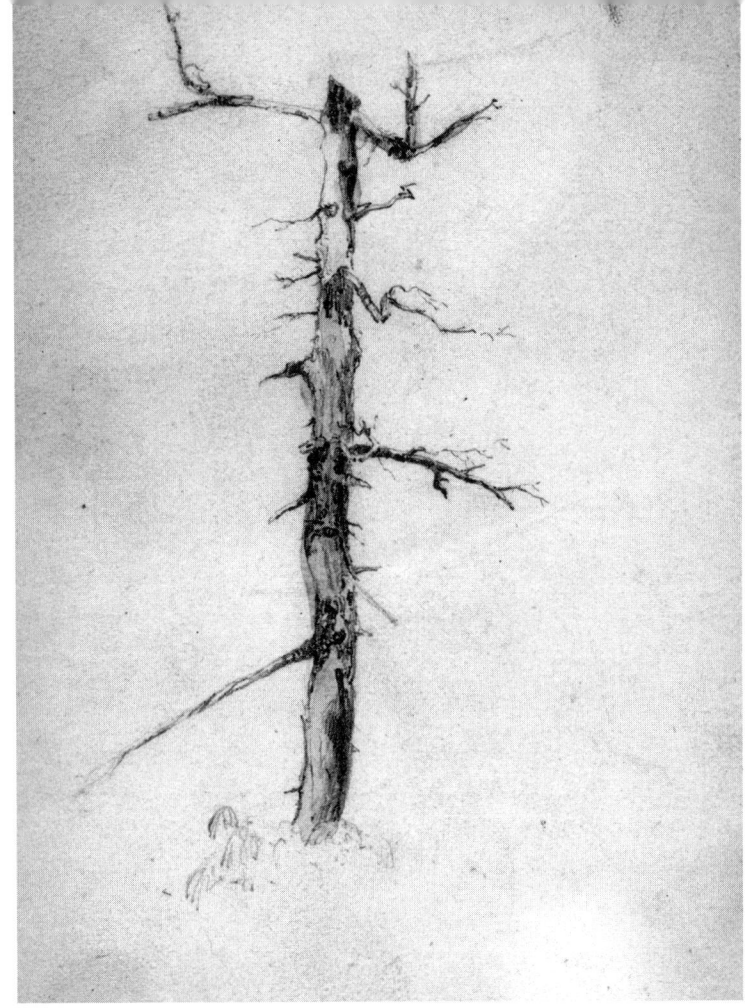

From the sketchbooks of B.B.G. Stone, 1854–1867.

THE LAUREL HOUSE

When the area prospered greatly from the summer vacation trade after the Civil War, the Schutt family more than doubled the size of the Laurel House with a right-angled addition featuring a plenitude of Victorian bracketed architecture. Never quite as ostentatious as either Hotel Kaaterskill or the Catskill Mountain House, Schutt's Laurel House near Kaaterskill Falls was a favorite with many artists. Its rates were less expensive and its season was longer. A *Recorder* news item on November 6, 1874, mentions that "The distinguished artists S.R. Gifford and Jervis McEntee, with Calvert Vaux, left Laurel House last week. B.B.G. Stone came down on Saturday."

The Schutts had hotel management in their blood. A forebear, Peter Schutt, in about 1823 operated an inn on the road from Catskill to Saugerties. Gallt in *Dear Old Greene County* states that

The Laurel House

The Laurel House was smaller than the Mountain House or Hotel Kaaterskill, but it was the closest to Kaaterskill Falls. The original structure was enlarged to accommodate guests seeking room and board at lower rates than those offered by the Laurel House's more famous competitors. Stereoview by J. Loeffler, Catskill Mountain Scenery, *first series.*

Grand Hotels and Private Parks

This stereoview from the top of Kaaterskill Falls looking down the glen in the early 1870s shows the pulley and pole device that lowered a bucket with liquid refreshments and picnic food to those below.

The Laurel House

Peter also had an interest in a Catskill village hotel in the early decades of the nineteenth century. Peter acquired a sizeable tract of land on the mountaintop that included Kaaterskill Falls itself, and he built a summer hotel and the tourist shanty overlooking the falls. (He always looked upon Haines Falls as a smaller, less distinguished rival.)

In the next generation J. Louis Schutt earned a livelihood in the hotel trade, as did Louis P. Schutt and James Schutt in the third generation. A fourth generation followed them in the trade. They could be found as far north as the Bethel Inn in Maine during the summer months and at Key West in the wintertime. Between the years 1913 to 1921, Louis P. Schutt managed Twilight Inn in Twilight Park. Some of his other managerial enterprises were Casa Marina at Key West, Hotel Ormand at Ormand Beach, and Long Key Fishing Camp.

All three sons of Louis P. Schutt were born at the Laurel House. George, the oldest son, was born in 1882. At the age of twelve, George was earning money as a bellboy at his relatives' hotel, the Catskill Mountain House.[1] After four years he was moved up to the front office as a mail clerk. In December 1899 he went to Nassau in the Bahamas for the Florida East Coast Hotel Company. Subsequently his father, who was then managing the Long Key Fishing Camp, secured work for George as a cashier and room clerk at the camp. He succeeded his father as fishing camp manager after his father was transferred to Casa Marina at Key West. This fishing camp attracted many sport fishermen, including novelist Zane Grey. George's brother Frank operated the Hotel Peabody in Memphis, Tennessee, for many years. All received their early training at the Laurel House.

The Laurel House was auctioned and purchased by Jacob Fromer in 1890, who leased the property until 1920, when it was purchased by Bunting and Bernstein. Eventually Nat Bernstein became the sole owner. Nat and his bride, Sadie, celebrated their wedding with a midnight dinner at the hotel on September 4, 1925. Bernstein sold the property in 1954 to two sisters—Mrs. Caldwell and Mrs. Curella. After closing the hotel on August 15, 1965, the sisters held an auction and then sold the building and its surrounding 105.5 acres to the State of New York, which added the property to the Catskill State Park. The state burned the Laurel House to the ground on February 27, 1967.

A color brochure in the final years advertises "A magnificent holiday resort 2400 feet above sea level in the beautiful Catskill Mountains," and stresses that "The Laurel House is located right at magnificent Kaaterskill Falls" and is "Only two-and-a-half hours from New York City. Please make reservations well in advance." Cardinal and Carella were the managers at that time, and the menu featured Italian-American cuisine. A cocktail lounge, outdoor swimming pool and

GRAND HOTELS AND PRIVATE PARKS

This 20th-century winter view of the Laurel House shows its nearness to Kaaterskill Falls. Note the platform at the top of the falls from which refreshments were lowered to customers waiting below.

evening dancing were further attractions. No rates were quoted in the brochure.

Notices posted in each room informed guests that a rising bell was rung at 7:30 AM with breakfast from 8:00 until 9:00 AM. Dinner was at 1:00 PM and a supper was served at 6:00 PM. The snack bar served food and coffee all day long.

Paper and other items connected with the Laurel House, such as the brochure and room notice quoted above, are highly collectible today.

The dam above Kaaterskill Falls, circa 1910. The Laurel House proprietors, for a nominal charge, would open the sluice gate to increase the flow of water over the falls.

From the sketchbooks of B.B.G. Stone, 1854–1867.

GUESTS AT THE MOUNTAIN HOUSE, 1922

Gone were the railroad connections from Catskill Point. Motorcar transportation was now the means of traveling the fifteen miles from Catskill to the Mountain House. Guests using the Ulster and Delaware Railroad's new, wider tracks were met by the hotel's motor bus.

The hotel's brochure claimed, "The new state road from Palenville to Haines Falls, with a grade not exceeding 8% is now open and offers the traveler a marvelous vista of the mountains and the valley en route to the Hotel." The booklet also contained a road map from metropolitan New York City to the Catskill Mountain House and offered a larger, more detailed one upon request.

As in prior brochures, photographic illustrations were featured: a frontal full view of the piazza with protective iron railings, the forest-shaded wooden walkway to South Lake, the casino, the tennis courts and other park views. A somewhat dated photo shows the interior ballroom with female guests in long, daytime dresses. The expansive view of the Hudson Valley was still a selling feature and was given prominence across the two center pages.

The promotional brochure circa 1922 carried John K. Van Wagonen's name as manager. The brochure's slogan was, "The Place For Your Summer Home Or To

Guests at the Mountain House, 1922

Alligator Rock, sometimes referred to as Whale Rock, is a natural rock formation near the Mountain House site. Note the small stones added to give the alligator its teeth. Postcard, c. 1892.

Side view of Kaaterskill Falls, 1871, with a good view of the platform and the pulley and basket.

Guests at the Mountain House, 1922

Spend Your Vacation." The booklet did not quote rates. For the convenience of guests from the New York City metropolitan area, an arrangement was made so that Mountain House reservations could be booked at the Hotel McAlpin in New York City.[1]

The brochure was more artistic than previous efforts, with a framed frontal illustration of the hotel and its site. The green cover contained embossed lettering and a logo consisting of interconnected Catskill Mountain House initials and decorative pinecones.

Having faced the reality of the need for modern plumbing, the owners had managed to raise the necessary capital to install a number of private baths. Gone were the washbowl and pitcher sets. Each bedroom now had hot and cold running water. Baths were also to be found on each floor, to be shared by guests in the less expensive rooms without private facilities. Good sanitation was stressed.

The "commodious dining room" could now seat 350 persons with many tables looking out on the famous view. As in prior decades special arrangements were available for governesses and their charges, who now had a separate dining room "with simple home cooked foods." The hours of meals were no longer specified.

Service conveniences were more numerous. The hotel now had its own post office with the address of Beachview, New York, with two daily deliveries and pickups. Telegrams were a fading practice, but the hotel now had long distance telephone connections. A house physician was "always in attendance," which might have meant that a nearby mountaintop doctor could be readily called in, or else a semiretired physician was given "free" room and board. Male barbers and female hairdressers were on duty, as well as a valet and a stenographer.

The usual recreational features now included a handball court, a casino with billiard and pool tables, and "first class bowling alleys." The old boathouse on South Lake had been replaced with a modern building that also was used for music and dancing. The ballroom was still in use for concerts and dances, with music "rendered by a well-known New York Orchestra." Other diversions included horse riding and motoring. A small, clock golf course had been added, modeled after an English putting game where players putt to a center hole from clock numbers circling a putting green.

Newspapers could be purchased at a main hall newsstand, which also was well-stocked with souvenirs. Postcards featuring the hotel and its environs had long been available.

Whether the early 1920s were as busy as earlier decades, with hardly a room to spare, is uncertain and probably doubtful. The warning that the "increased popularity of the Mountain House makes early reservations advisable, as during past seasons it has been impossible to accommodate all who wish to sojourn here" may have been included to firm up bookings to assist the hotel owners in planning the summer.

From the sketchbooks of B.B.G. Stone, 1854–1867.

THE MOUNTAIN HOUSE FOR SALE

From the time of the death of her father, Charles L. Beach, in 1902, Sarah Avery Beach held a one-third interest in the Catskill Mountain House Company. Behind the scenes she was active in its management, but in public she deferred to her two brothers, George H. and Charles Beach. When the Catskill Mountain House Company was dissolved in 1910, the new corporation carried the name Charles and George H. Beach & Company. After the death of Charles in 1913, the firm carried on as George H. Beach & Company. Sarah Beach was the "& Company." George died in 1918 leaving his widow, Ida Gardiner Beach, as his heir. George and Ida had been married in 1880; there were two offspring.

With her husband's death in 1913, Martha Congdon Beach (Mrs. Charles Beach) had assumed control of one-third of the Catskill Mountain House property. With the declining success of the hotel as it entered the second decade of the twentieth century, Martha decided to sell her one-third interest in the Mountain

The Mountain House for Sale

House lands and buildings as well as her interest in and to "all the household goods and furniture, supplies, machines, machinery, tools, implements, horses, cattle, swine, poultry, carriages, sleighs, automobiles, harness, hay, straw and grain, and all other chattel property now upon and used in connection with the lands and premises, which are known as the Catskill Mountain House property." The buyers were Sarah and Ida Beach. The sale took place on January 14, 1924, and the purchase price was $20,000. Unable to pay with cash, the buyers signed a second mortgage claim. Later, Martha sold that mortgage to her relatives, Belle and Beulah Barkley.

Sarah and Ida now each held a 50 percent interest in the Catskill Mountain House property. The two ladies carried on the operation of the hotel, hiring John K. Van Wagonen as manager. Van Wagonen was a son-in-law of Ida Beach, and his wife, Mary L. Beach Van Wagonen, was Sarah's niece.

In the next few years, faced with an aging resort and declining patronage, the financial condition of the Catskill Mountain House continued to deteriorate. Both ladies had signed promissory notes for operating capital, including the interest on the two mortgages. Should they lease or sell? Advice was sought from several quar-

The Catskill Mountain Railroad was developed by Charles L. Beach and Associates to compete with the Ulster and Delaware and Stony Clove route from Kingston to the mountaintop. The first engine was a Schenectady locomotive purchased to haul shale brick. It was destroyed in the repair shop fire and replaced by this engine.

Winter view from Sunset Rock, 1880s.

The Mountain House for Sale

ters, including that of L.P. Schutt, who was married to a sister of Ida and was experienced in the operation of resort property.

The two ladies also met with the family's Catskill law firm of Osborn, Bloodgood, Wilbur and Fray.[1] The latter, in response to an inquiry from Schutt, informed him that:

> Miss Sarah Beach and Mrs. Ida Beach have asked our advice at different times in reference to the sale of the Catskill Mountain House Property, or some part of it, and while it is hard for them to think of letting the property pass out of their family after so many years of Beach ownership, it seems to us (and we have so advised them) that the responsibility of managing such a large property is too much for two ladies to carry. They have finally authorized us today to offer the property for sale, including the personal property in the hotel of which they have an inventory, for $150,000, except the small parcel between the highway leading from the hotel to Haines Falls and the old road known as Scribner Road.

More immediately pressing than the sale of the Catskill Mountain House was the need for the law firm to gain a better understanding of the numerous outstanding accounts owed by the business. For this information they turned to hotel manager John K. Van Wagonen, who had the books and papers in his possession. One of the larger creditors was Van Wagonen himself, who was still owed $750.00 on his 1927 salary. Next were the insurance bills held by T. B. Beach & Company, amounting to $700.63. The other creditors were from Kingston, Catskill, Haines Falls, Tannersville and Hunter for various smaller amounts. The list prepared in December 1927 included the Jacob Forst Packing Company for meat supplied to the hotel, amounting to $539.30, and the firms of Day & Holt, Geo. W. Holdridge, Haines Garage, Doyle's Garage, Schoharie Telephone Company, L.S. Winnie and Haines Market. Individual claims of Alfred Legg and Robert Terns could be partially offset by their purchases of lumber. Worthy Speenburg (acting as hotel caretaker) was owed one month's salary in the amount of $65.00 plus the costs of five bushels of potatoes, one hundred pounds of flour, the shoeing of horses and repairs to the brake. The electric bill had been kept current except for the last month's charge of $1.44. Sixty cords of wood supplied by John Lewis and Jerry Linzey amounted to $150.00. The total debts stood at $2,937.48.

Seeking to collect money owed to George H. Beach & Company, the law firm secured an O.H. Perry note for $1,500.00 which, when discounted, paid off Van Wagonen's arrears in salary and the insurance premiums. Still owing were William

France ($24.22), Henry Hansen ($128.30), O.H. Perry ($421.54), Mrs. R.W. Renner ($17.43), Lawrence Schoonmaker ($120.88), Mrs. Howards ($38.20), The Antlers Hotel ($121.98), Charles Layman ($177.80), and Mrs. Lee W. Higgins of Onteora Park "now in Europe" ($90.00). This list was later amended to include the Tannersville Supply Company ($94.22) and the Loxhurst ($36.88). By December 19, debtors Schoonmaker, Tannersville Supply Company, Lucy Martin Myer (the Loxhurst), and C.B. Layman had liquidated their debt.

Looking ahead to the hotel season of 1928, the law firm attempted to forecast operating costs. Between December 1, 1927, and April 1, 1928, George H. Beach & Company had to pay out $4,500.00 broken down as follows:

> Martha C. Beach's mortgage interest, $600.00
> Ice-harvesting expenses, $300.00
> Town of Catskill taxes, $1,650.00
> Town of Hunter taxes, $150.00
> Wages of caretaker for four months, $260.00
> 150 cords of wood, $400.00
> Catskill Savings Bank interest on mortgage, $900.00
> Interest on notes endorsed, $140.00
> Feed for horses, $100.00

Over the winter of 1927-28, Sarah and Ida, unable to sell, considered other possibilities, none of which met with the approval of their law firm. On April 30, 1928, attorneys wrote to Sarah:

> We cannot say to you, as it would not be a frank and honest expression of our opinion that we approve of the plan proposed by you in writing to us this morning with reference to the Mountain House. We believe it would result in a substantial depreciation of the value of the property ... We have not changed in the least the views we expressed to you several months ago about the Mountain House property. You and Mrs. Ida Beach have simply disagreed with our views and preferred not to accept our advice or suggestions, and of course you both had the right to do so if you felt that we were mistaken in our judgment. It would seem that the situation has since become still more unfavorable.

The letter went on to urge the two owners to seek the advice of a disinterested businessman.

The Mountain House for Sale

Hiking party resting at Sunset Rock, 1880s. Note the walking sticks.

The Layman Memorial, commemorating the Haines Falls man who lost his life fighting a forest fire on South Mountain on August 10, 1900.

The Mountain House for Sale

A long conference was held with Ida on May 14, 1928, at the law office. Sarah was not present. Out of that session came a letter to Sarah outlining the only courses of action possible.

1. You can hire a manager, furnish him with money to open the hotel for the coming season, and authorize him to go ahead with the business;
2. You can lease the property to anyone, and upon such terms and conditions as you see fit;
3. You can determine not to take either of the courses already suggested, and instead of doing so advertise the property for sale at private sale and wait for some prospective purchaser to come forward and negotiate.
4. You can advertise the property for sale at public auction, giving it wide publicity, and sell it to the highest bidder. And the public sale can be had early in June.

It is our opinion that a sale of the property at public auction would be better for you and Mrs. Beach than either of the other courses we have suggested. BUT YOU SHOULD COME TO SOME DECISION NOW, AND SHOULD NOT ALLOW THIS IMPORTANT MATTER TO DRIFT ALONG AS IT HAS BEEN DOING FOR SEVERAL MONTHS.

The letter from Osborn, Bloodgood, Wilbur and Fray had an immediate effect. On May 17, 1928, Sarah and Ida signed and delivered the following letter:

Dear Sirs:

We are satisfied after much reflection that we should not undertake to conduct the Mountain House business any longer, as we cannot give it personal attention. The condition of our health will not permit. The property has been in the Beach family for many years, and we have wanted to keep it, and manage or lease it. But since you disapprove of leasing we have decided to sell the property, and therefore want to put it in your hands for that purpose. Please take such steps as you think necessary or advisable to make an early sale of all the real estate, and all the hotel furniture and furnishings, either at public or private sale.

Unfortunately no buyer surfaced and no auction was held. The Catskill Mountain House opened for the 1928 season still owned by the Beaches and managed by John K. Van Wagonen.

From the sketchbooks of B.B.G. Stone, 1854–1867.

THE MOUNTAIN HOUSE UNDER VAN WAGONEN OWNERSHIP

In the early months of 1929, the two Mountain House heirs, Louis and Charles Beach, great-nephews of the legendary Charles L. Beach (1808-1902), builder of the Catskill Mountain House, saw little future in trying to maintain and operate an aging summer hotel. The hotel was long on history and tradition, but short on operating capital. Faced with a heavy burden of debt in the form of two mortgages, Louis and Charles were ready to accept John K. Van Wagonen's offer of $20,000 for their shares of stock in the Catskill Mountain House. It was not even a cash offer. Van Wagonen would sign six promissory notes staggered over the next three years and secured by a third mortgage.

The Mountain House under Van Wagonen Ownership

There is still some confusion as to the shares issued by the reincorporated Catskill Mountain House Company. The stock record book has not surfaced. In any event neither Sarah nor Ida Beach would have caused Van Wagonen any problems, their relationship being a close one. Van Wagonen's wife was Mary L. Beach, Ida's daughter. Both Sarah (in 1934) and Ida (in 1936) would pass away at the Van Wagonen home at 23 King Street, Catskill.

How realistic was Van Wagonen in making the offer to purchase? Since the early 1920s, first as assistant manager and later as manager and vice president, he had first-hand experience in feeding, housing and entertaining summer guests at a time when the automobile was changing America's vacation patterns. He was knowledgeable about the hotel's debts and the two mortgages. Probably the most

The stairway to the bottom of the first level at Kaaterskill Falls. The lack of flowing water indicates a dry season. Postcard, c. 1910.

Sunset Rock, approximately 1700 feet above the clove floor. Twilight Park can be seen in the distance. Postcard c. 1910.

important factor influencing his decision was the pending sale of four-fifths of the Pine Orchard lands to the State of New York. On September 10, 1929, Van Wagonen made his final decision—he would purchase.

The part played in Van Wagonen's decision by his wife Mary can only be surmised. As the granddaughter of Charles L. Beach, Mary must have been pleased to see the family tradition carried on. She could look back to June 29, 1911, when an elaborate wedding reception was held for her and John in the ballroom of the Catskill Mountain House. That event had included a special train from Catskill where the wedding was held, an orchestra from New York City, a searchlight trained on landmarks in the valley, and superb food.

There almost was a last-minute snag to the sale when Louis informed Van Wagonen by letter that on July 28, 1928, he had executed an assignment of 390 shares of the corporation stock to his son Raymond. Apparently the transfer was never completed, however, and the newly issued shares of stock remained in the stock transfer book. Louis wrote that "I am still the sole owner of said 400 shares." His offer to "save harmless" Van Wagonen resolved the problem and led to Van Wagonen signing the six promissory notes.

On the evening of September 23, 1929, the Catskill Mountain House board of directors met, with John Fray of the law firm of Osborn, Bloodgood, Wilbur and Fray providing legal direction. The first order of business was to accept the resignation of Louis Beach as a director. Virgil B. Van Wagonen (John's son) was voted in. The next order of business was to accept a similar resignation from Charles Beach as director and the filling of that vacancy by John Van Wagonen's daughter Maggie.

Next came the election of officers. Louis and Charles resigned as president and as secretary-treasurer, respectively. John Van Wagonen was removed as vice president, but only so as to take on the corporate presidency. Virgil became vice president as well as treasurer, while Maggie agreed to serve as secretary. The Beaches were out, and the Van Wagonen family was in control of the Catskill Mountain House.

That same evening, in the Catskill law office of Osborn, Bloodgood, Wilbur and Fray, the new directors of the Catskill Mountain House, as part of the purchase and sale agreement, gave their consent to a mortgage in favor of Louis and Charles Beach. This covered the hotel's main building, outbuildings, and parcels of land, as well as a chattel claim on all of the corporation's personal property including furniture, equipment, linens, dishes, even pots and pans. This was the third mortgage, and it was subject to the prior claims of the Catskill Savings Bank's first mortgage and the second mortgage held by Belle and Beulah Barkley.

From the sketchbooks of B.B.G. Stone, 1854–1867.

MOUNTAIN HOUSE FINALE

John Van Wagonen might have succeeded in his operational plans for the Catskill Mountain House had it not been for the economic crash of 1929 and the Great Depression. Vacations suddenly became a luxury most people could not afford. The Mountain House became insolvent and was acquired by Tannersville banker Milo Claude Moseman and his associate, attorney Clyde Gardiner, who leased the hotel to the Andron family of New York City. Moseman later bought out Gardiner's share and acquired sole proprietorship of the aging resort.

Global events, however, doomed Moseman's efforts to revive the grand hotel.[1] World War II followed fast on the heels of the Depression, and few vacationers frequented the Catskills during the war years. The Mountain House's long, slow decline now spiraled out of control. By mid-century the structure was in serious trouble:

> The Catskill Mountain House is falling to pieces. The five Greek Revival pediments once rested on thirteen Corinthian columns. Now only five remain together with a

Mountain House Finale

Winter view of Kaaterskill Clove looking west from the Laurel House, c. 1877.

few emergency props. Once again it is obvious that private ownership is unable to support one of New York State's, indeed one of the country's outstanding landmarks. Help by public agencies or interested societies must be sought.

This was the opening paragraph of a letter published in *The New York Times* on November 20, 1951, written by Hans Muth of the Art Institute of Chicago. The letter writer went on to detail the history of the Catskill Mountain House and its significance to the Hudson River School, especially to Thomas Cole who "could observe the site from the piazza of his house [in Catskill]; he painted it frequently and was one of those who contributed greatly to making the magnificent site well known." Muth ended with the warning: "But it is necessary to hurry else the building will fall into complete ruin this winter, and the Hudson Valley will be deprived of one of its most impressive features."

Six days later Muth wrote to a friend in Catskill assumed to be one of the Beach family lawyers. "In case you have not read the letter I addressed to the *Times* and which this paper was good enough to print on November 20, I enclose a copy of it. I received a number of enthusiastic replies. ... But naturally the main thing is what does the owner think about it?" Muth went on to express his fervent hope that this communication would soon reach the legal owner of the Catskill Mountain House, whose name and address he did not know.

In this roundabout manner the letter did reach Moseman. On December 21 Moseman replied:

Dear Mr. Muth,

Your letter sent to your friend in Catskill to be addressed and sent to the owner of the Catskill Mountain House came to me. As owner of this property and as one having a much deeper affection for the property than the presence of the building would indicate I was more than pleased with your article on the editorial page of the *New York Times* of the November 20th issue. It was my purpose then to write you a letter of appreciation realizing that you were one who had grasped the significance of this old land

Mountain House Finale

The piazza of the Catskill Mountain House, early spring 1961. Photograph by Roland Van Zandt. © Black Dome Press Corp.

mark. For the past month most of my time has been required in Court, however, while in New York on one occasion I went to the *Times* Office at West 43rd Street and purchased one hundred copies of the issue, and have all of them in my office with the idea of using them as soon as I can find a period that can be devoted for a few days just to the Mountain House. What you have suggested, I too, have wanted for some time and now want. One of my dreams will be realized should some people or agencies acquire this property wholly conscious of its legend, tradition and history and so treat the property in a manner for the future, worthy of its institution.

I unqualifiedly approve and give you my personal permission as the sole owner of the Catskill Mountain House to push the matter a little further as you indicated and send copies of your thoughts for its present and future coincides very much with mine, as mine have been expressed through the columns of several of our local papers in the so-called capital district of this state, which comprises Albany, Schoharie, Columbia, Dutchess, Ulster, Rensselaer and Greene. I think it is pretty well known in this area that I want to preserve the old portion of the house which will include the lobby with its adjacent living rooms, the souvenir room, a portion of the dining room, the ball room and approximately thirty five bedrooms. With this idea in mind I have recently sold the wings to be removed. The northerly wing particularly will give further access and approach to the view from the north, which has not been possible for many years. That which I have retained, I am sure will be adequate and sufficient for the purpose such as you outlined in your letter. I will be glad to quote you a price after we have had some further interchange of letters. I assure you that any price that I will fix will be reasonable. It positively will not be huge or excessive.

Having been born in the Catskills, I have known of this property for more than forty five years and I have been quite close to it in many ways and it is suffice to say that I have been affected by it personally, even though it be but a material thing. However, there is no spot that I know where there is more awe inspiring manifestation of nature than on the cliff of the Catskill Mountain House.

I shall look forward to letters from you and that we may not overlap I would be glad to be provided with a list of the agencies to whom you send a copy of your letter. I assure you that I will have no communication with any of them unless sought through you, excepting I expect to use the one hundred which I have in my office.

Mountain House Finale

The front of the Catskill Mountain House, summer 1962. The New York State Conservation Department had removed the piazza and the remaining columns. Photograph by Roland Van Zandt. © Black Dome Press Corp.

> Again I want to express my deep appreciation because there is something more than material in this matter and it is that which is not material which is of the most profound interest to me.

Moseman's hope to save the Catskill Mountain House was not to be. His visionary dream of a Catskill Mountain House preserved for future generations was a few decades too early for success. The historic preservation movement was just beginning, with limited federal and state financial assistance available. The physical deterioration of the building as witnessed by Muth continued, although Moseman's decision to remove the north and south wings was a practical response to a difficult situation. It was suggested by some that the Greene County Historical Society take on the restoration effort, but in 1960 that small not-for-profit educational corporation was already deeply committed to raising funds for major restoration efforts on its several-building complex known as the Bronck Homestead. (Decades later the society did take on the burden of the badly deteriorated Cedar Grove—Thomas Cole's house in Catskill—when all other avenues failed.)

The final years of Moseman's life saw the sale of much of the Mountain House lands to the Carpathian Vacation Camp, Inc. Subsequent to his death, his heirs sold the remaining acreage and the ruins of the building itself to the same corporation. Its planned summer bungalow colony never materialized, and in 1962 title passed to the State of New York. Today, together with the Hotel Kaaterskill acreage and the Laurel House property, this is one of the state's most popular Catskill Mountains hiking and camping areas.

On the morning of Friday, January 25, 1963, at 6:00 AM, the New York State Department of Conservation set fire to the ruins of the Catskill Mountain House. Its farewell was eloquently sounded in an Annabar Jensis editorial in the Catskill *Daily Mail:*

> The Mountain House died hard. She was too lovely, and too proud to fall into decay. She was weathered and tumbled and ravaged by fire, but still she stood, defying the elements of the windswept mountaintop. She had to die because her rotted beams endangered the thousands who came to pay homage, who could not resist the temptation to approach her and peer through her darkened windows.
>
> The Mountain House died by fire in the dawn of a bitter morning. Her passing was noted as far away as Catskill, where one man saw the blaze and thought, for one awful moment, that the sun was rising in the west, so red

was the glow on the horizon. Her death was mourned by man; her executioners were in the long run, time; and in the short run, the men from the State Conservation Dept. who eased her leave-taking from this world.

Thousands of ghosts—presidents, senators, crowned heads of European royalty—will also mourn her passing. Thousands of feet trod her halls, walked to the edge of the precipice and rambled the paths which surrounded her. Thousands of eyes thrilled to her many-columned loveliness; thousands of ears were soothed by the music of the orchestras which played softly in her ballroom.

Those of us who were too young to have seen her in her beauty have been deprived, by an accident of time, of a magnificent sight. Let us remember her as she was: as a white-pillared elegance looking over the mountain and valley; as a weathered crone clinging to life as long as she was permitted to live; and, lastly, as a vast sheet of flame bringing wonder and fear to all who saw it.

This was the Mountain House—and something great has fallen.

From the sketchbooks of B.B.G. Stone, 1854–1867.

HOMES NEAR TO NATURE

Small summer cottages or camps, some of which are still in use today, developed in the northern Catskills in the years after 1880. Associations of summer dwellers came into being, providing road maintenance, a common water supply, a resident caretaker and clubhouse services. Among these mountaintop "cooperatives" were Elka Park, Onteora Park, Santa Cruz Park, Twilight Park and Sunset Park. The latter three are located at the head of Kaaterskill Clove.

Santa Cruz Park later merged with Twilight Park, while the Sunset Park Association eventually was dissolved as a legal entity. The Sunset Hotel, under private ownership, continued to provide lodging and dining facilities for summer vacationers.

In driving up the Kaaterskill Clove state highway (Route 23A) one gets a quick view of buildings clinging to the steep mountainside. One such Santa Cruz (Spanish for "Holy Cross") rustic cottage was Tree Tops, the summer home of Charles H. Lounsbury of Connecticut. In 1912 Edward F. Bigelow, managing editor of the illustrated monthly magazine *The Guide to Nature* published by the Agassiz Association, was a guest of Lounsbury. Out of that summer experience came the

Homes near to Nature

Kaaterskill Clove as viewed from Twilight Park's Ledge End Inn.

article "The Switzerland of America" with the message to "See America First."[1]

Tree Tops had a half-log natural siding on the outside, while inside was a combination of narrow, varnished tongue-and-groove boards with an arched, natural stone fireplace as the living room's focal point. The furnishings were typical of summer cottages at the turn of the twentieth century: sisal-type rugs, hardwood rocking chairs and wicker pieces. Lighting came from kerosene lamps, with one hanging from the ceiling. There was much

In the Sitting Room of "Tree Tops," *from Edward F. Bigelow's article, "The Switzerland of America," in* The Guide to Nature, *September 1912.*

Homes near to Nature

The Summer House in the Dense Foliage, *from Edward F. Bigelow's article, "The Switzerland of America," in* The Guide to Nature, *September 1912.*

"artistic clutter" on the walls, mantel, reading and tea tables.

The Lounsburys apparently spent many hours outdoors in an open-sided structure on a mountainside spot sheltered from the hot rays of the summer sun by dense foliage. For the more venturesome there were bypaths and dirt roadways to nearby places of scenic beauty.

The view down Kaaterskill Clove from Tree Tops' veranda was described in Bigelow's article:

> One may look east and like a bird see the valley, down, down, so far below that the tree tops are far beneath the observer, and so densely massed

Ledge End Inn in Twilight Park provided lodging and meals. Cottage owners as well as hotel guests frequented the dining room. Postcard, c. 1920.

Haines Falls. Stereoview by W.H. Towne, Lansingburgh, N.Y., 1880s.

Grand Hotels and Private Parks

The private resort colony of Twilight Park in winter. Photograph by S. Elmer Davis, Catskill, March 2, 1898.

together that the eye cannot distinguish one tree from another, but blends them into one soft, deep, luxuriant canopy that covers in beautiful patterns of varying shades the entire valley, which slopes grandly upward the rounding mountaintop. To the east, gleaming like a silver arrow, lies the Hudson River, and far beyond rises the Berkshire mountains.

The Santa Cruz Inn, at that time managed by a Mrs. French, was a place of rest and refreshments for locals and summer guests. The Sunset Inn was recommended as a place where the veranda view was so inspiring that, in Bigelow's opinion, "the view from the northern veranda is awe-inspiring in the extreme. It is so grand that it never tires, and becomes monotonous. The pretty things of life become irksome, but grander duties and scenes have other and different functions."

In the final paragraph about Kaaterskill Clove, Bigelow wrote that "there are deeper gorges, greater streams and higher mountains but in no other place is the combination so blended into a harmony so perfect as to form such tempting bits for the camera or the brush."

B.B.G. Stone, Sunset Rock, *pencil drawing, 1888. This view looking west through Kaaterskill Clove towards Haines Falls is from the escarpment trail on South Mountain. The view today would include the cottages of Twilight Park to the left of the falls.*

V
Harvesting the Clove's Resources

Kaaterskill Clove has little or no tillable land. Early legends of gold and silver mines were told and retold, but the geological formation of the Catskills precludes such finds. The beauty of its scenery is and always has been the clove's greatest natural resource.

Other, more tangible resources did, however, draw some entrepreneurs to the clove. Its forests were thinned by lumbermen, tanners, and charcoal burners despite the clove's steep slopes, and its bluestone beds were quarried for paving stones.

From the sketchbooks of B.B.G. Stone, 1854–1867.

INDUSTRY IN THE CLOVE

Except for the hikers who leave the state highway at Moore's Bridge and walk along Kaaterskill Creek to a small, level, mostly overgrown stretch of land, few realize that this midsection of the clove was the location of a sizeable village known as East Hunter. The vanished village consisted of a cluster of workers' houses, a store, a post office and Kiersted's Tannery. It was a time of large families, so the local school had over two hundred young scholars. The Kaaterskill in those days was not the clear, flowing stream of today; it was quite polluted from the tannery operations. Thousands of hides were tanned and shipped out until the scarcity of hemlock bark closed the tannery, forcing the families to move away to seek employment elsewhere, leaving behind a deserted village and tannery. Today, foundation ruins and a large metal water pipe are the sole reminders of East Hunter village. There is a good possibility that the workers' small houses might have been company houses, since at least fifteen were eventually sold, dismantled, and transported to the village of Catskill, where they were re-erected at Joesburgville, a humorous newspaper label

Industry in the Clove

Early view of the Palenville entrance to Kaaterskill Clove, 1850s. The building immediately to the left of the bridge eventually was converted into an artist's studio by George H. Hall. A tollbooth is visible farther up the clove road.

Harvesting the Clove's Resources

for the stretch of the Athens (Albany and Greene) Turnpike as it climbed the steep hill.

Hotels and boardinghouses surrounded the clove and were operated on a seasonal basis. Brockett's in the Clove had a much longer season, almost year-round.

On the mountaintop and close to the clove were the locations of several Haines family establishments, one of the most prominent being that of Mr. and Mrs. Charles Haines. Their large boardinghouse closed down in August of 1895 after the sudden death of Mr. Haines. Nicknamed "Christian Charley," Haines was then sixty-five years of age and for years had been prominent in church and temperance work, and had been a delegate to the state convention of the Prohibition Party. He was an abolitionist before the Civil War, and subsequently was a generous contributor

Stone foundation walls are all that remain of the tannery at East Hunter Village, upstream from Moore's Bridge. The tannery closed when hemlock bark became scarce. Photograph by Harvey Durham, April 28, 1992.

toward the education of the freed African-Americans. He was always proud of the falls that carried his family name.[1]

The hotel was sold to the New York City firm of Cantwell and Davis, and operated in the summers under the management of J.J. Burns, also of New York. The structure, insured for $27,000, was destroyed by fire in 1911.

Bluestone quarries furnished stone for the building industry and for sidewalks until the use of Portland cement became commonplace. The stone varied in color and required the removal of at least several feet of rock and shale before the bed could be mined. Several quarries in the clove and around the base of the mountains provided seasonal employment, but not to the extent found at the quarries in West Saugerties. The *Examiner* carried one firm's advertisement in its November 16, 1872, issue:

> CATSKILL MOUNTAIN BLUESTONE—G. & S. I. Griffin, at Palenville, Greene Co., NY are prepared to fill orders for Flagging, Curb Gutters, Cross-Walks, Platforms, Sills, Lintels and Coping, of the best quality of Mountain Stone. Also Rubbed Hearths, Tile, Water Table Sills, Lintels and all the varieties of rubbed stone, furnished from their Polishing Works at short notice. Stone trimmed, ready for the masons.

By the early decades of the twentieth century, there are known to have been six operating quarries—two in the clove itself and four at the base of South Mountain. J.H. Wolven had his quarry on the north side of Kaaterskill Clove, five hundred feet above the creek bed and about two and three-quarter miles west of Palenville. By removing thirty to thirty-five feet of top deposits, including shale, he and his four men mined a bed of stone, eight feet in thickness; the slabs were hoisted by means of a hand derrick. As the workmen hauled the product up from the quarry, they were occasionally reminded of the geological formation of the Catskills when they sighted a reed fossil. Wolven reported that he was taking out from six to seven loads of stone per week, his wagons and teams hauling the loads fifteen miles to the Ulster Bluestone Company's Hudson River docks at Malden.

The Hommel and Rightmeyer quarry was on the opposite side of the clove canyon almost across from Wolven's. Their bed was described as "thinner in nature, some three feet." Two men were employed during the eight-month season. Their stone also was hauled to Malden.

With the easier woodlands already harvested, attention shifted to more difficult forests such as in the clove's upper reaches. For one operation a chute made of logs bolted and keyed together was laid down the steep incline of the gorge a distance of 1 7/8 miles. The chute was constructed both on the ground and on trestle supports. Felled logs were shuttled down the chute to within a short distance of a sawmill set up in the clove at the foot of Horseshoe Curve. It took only seconds from the time the log was placed in the chute until it reached the lower end. Connected with the lumbering operation was a "camp village" of houses and barns where the lumbermen and their families lived. The sawmill itself was well equipped to dress the sawn lumber by planing and edging. It was estimated that this Kaaterskill Clove sawmill turned out 10,000 feet of lumber daily.

Another profitable forest product was charcoal. Charcoal was lightweight, easy to transport, and had a ready market. Hampton C. Randolph, whose parents had an older boardinghouse down below the Santa Cruz Inn, knew of charcoal burners who operated on the clove's mountains. In 1995 Randolph reminisced about seeing the ruins of a burner's cabin in the clove.

Industry in the Clove

Quarry owned by Pete and Uriah Haines, located high on Prospect Mountain near Sphinx Rock. Photograph c. 1890. The Mountain Top Historical Society.

From the sketchbooks of B.B.G. Stone, 1854–1867.

LOGGING THE PINE ORCHARD

In the early years after the death in 1902 of their father, Charles L. Beach, the three Beach heirs—Sarah and her brothers, George and Charles—were faced not only with the necessity of raising more capital for their Catskill Mountain House operations, but also of meeting the costs of their comfortable lifestyles that included winter months in southern resorts. One of their first moves was to dissolve the Catskill Mountain House Company, which their father had incorporated under New York State law in March 1871 with an authorized capital stock of 500 shares at a face value of $25,000. The dissolution came in

Logging the Pine Orchard

May of 1910. The papers filed stated that the Catskill Mountain House Company had paid no dividends that year. The three heirs also could not expect much, if anything, from their First Income Bonds of the Catskill Mountain Railway, of which Sarah held $33,500, Charles $30,500, and George $28,000—no small sums in those years.

The extensive acreage that Charles L. Beach had developed for a driving and walking park surrounding his pillared Catskill Mountain House had furnished some timber and firewood in earlier years, but still contained mature spruce trees capable of yielding millions of board-feet of lumber. The problem posed in harvesting this potential source of additional income was not to use a heavy-handed cutover method, but rather a selective cutting that would preserve much of the park-like atmosphere of the Pine Orchard. Could the Beach family find a contractor who would be sensitive to the problem and yet be able to make a profit on such a restrictive logging contract? The Beach heirs thought they had found one in O.H Perry of Fort Plain, New York.

Then there was the matter of the longstanding mortgage held by the Catskill Savings Bank, whose officers were increasingly unwilling to release its claim without some reduction in the mortgage, which now stood at $30,000. The legal work dragged on as a restrictive logging contract was drawn up by the Catskill law firm of Osborn, Bloodgood & Wilbur. At the time of signing, only George was in Greene County. Sarah was in North Carolina, and Charles and his wife Martha were sojourning in Florida. The contract became binding on December 11, 1912. The eleven-page legal document furnishes the reader of today with substantial local history.[1]

Section 1 of the contract states:

> The first parties [Beach heirs] herewith sell unto the said second party [O.H. Perry] and the second party hereby purchases of the first parties all the spruce standing timber, measuring eight inches or more in diameter, three feet from the ground, on that certain track of land belonging to the parties of the first part situated in the town of Hunter (or partially in the town of Hunter and partially in the town of Catskill), Greene County, New York, containing about ten hundred and twenty acres more or less, and adjoining the upper or North Lake.

There were two restrictions on the 1,020 acres mentioned in the contract. Excepted from harvesting were all spruce trees on the west slope of North Mountain, and any trees standing within fifty feet of North Lake.

Charles H. Van Orden, a Catskill civil engineer, was given the task of developing blueprints of the acres to be shorn of their spruce trees.

Using Baughman's Band Saw Log Scale, Perry was to pay for timber at the rate of eight dollars per thousand feet after the logs had been placed on skid ways at the sawmill. It also was understood that a caretaker for the Catskill Mountain House property could witness the measurements.

In harvesting the timber the work crew was required to fell the trees as close to the ground as possible to avoid any unnecessary waste. All logs not exceeding twenty feet in length were to be measured at the small end, while all exceeding twenty feet were to be measured in the center. Additionally, the end measurements were to be made within the bark, and the center measurements were to be made outside the bark.

Perry was required to cut at least two million board feet annually beginning January 1, 1913, and to continue until all spruce trees of the specified sizes were cut. Of importance to the Beach family were the monthly monetary installments beginning February 1913 for all timber cut during the preceding calendar month. Should Perry fail to cut less than one-twelfth of two million feet in any one month, payment for the larger amount was still due and payable.

Key to the successful timbering operation was the proximity of the Catskill and Tannersville Railroad for transporting the sawn lumber. The Beach heirs agreed to permit Perry to erect and operate a sawmill and its appurtenances on land lying between the railroad and the road leading from the Kaaterskill Station of the Ulster and Delaware to the highway running from the Catskill Mountain House to Haines Falls. Additionally a five-acre wood lot between the Catskill and Tannersville Railroad and the highway was made available if needed for log storage.

Three acres were available to provide housing for work crews and barns for horses and equipment. This lot was on the north side of the railroad and adjoined the southwest corner of the Mountain House's "Golf Barn Lot." Accommodations for no more than ten men, either a building or a tent, also could be erected on the east slope of the plateau known as the "Burnt District."

Fearful of the common practice of harvesting only the easier trees, the contract required Perry and his men to work outward from a center point of the tract "and continue his cutting at substantially an equal distance from that point in all directions." Log roads and, if necessary, railroads and cableways were permitted. Danger from fire was to be minimized and all water pipes were to be protected. The contract expressly prohibited the operation of any saloon, probably to the dismay of the workers. And finally, all the temporary buildings were to be removed within six months after the completion of the contract.

Mill ponds were a source of power for lumber processing.
This sawmill was near the Laurel House. Photograph, 1880s.

The two contracting parties were to make use of the Tanners National Bank. Payments were to be made payable to "Charles and George H. Beach & Company." Five thousand dollars was to be held in trust as a contract guarantee.

With the death of Charles Beach, overseeing the Perry lumber contract became the responsibility of his brother George. On June 17, 1914, a new contract was signed that addressed the failure to meet five months' payments to the new corporation, George H. Beach & Company.

On June 16, 1917, John K. Van Wagonen, then employed as assistant manager of the Catskill Mountain House, wrote to attorney Frank H. Osborn about the Perry contract, in which "he [Perry] has six months after the performance of his contract to remove said buildings and property." The Perry sawmill had stopped operating on August 5, 1916, and the last payment to balance the account was made on September 15, 1916. Gone was all the lumber of any value, but the engines, boiler, and lumberyard had not been cleaned up. In late winter or the early spring of 1917, the sides of the sawmill collapsed and the roof fell, covering the machinery. The smokestack held by guy ropes still stood, but with little underpinning. There was danger of its falling and injuring a passersby going to or from the Kaaterskill Station. Van Wagonen proposed a bond for $1,000 for cleaning up the property.

On February 8, 1919, Perry was notified that there was serious concern at his failure to remove the buildings and equipment under the contract of 1912. There was also an unsightly, large pile of sawdust at the site. Two days later Perry replied to Osborn, Bloodgood, Wilbur & Fray, stating that when he had left the mountaintop he had sold the mill to the Worm Brothers, junk dealers in Haines Falls. Perry was willing to release all claims to the machinery to Van Wagonen and further stated he would come down to resolve the other matters, which it appears he did because the correspondence between him and the Beach attorney terminated.

Logging the Pine Orchard

Small sawmills provided crude housing and meals for work crews. This postcard is dated October 12, 1908.

Kaaterskill-in-the-Catskills, N.Y. A Saw Mill and Camp in the heart of the Catskills.

From the sketchbooks of B.B.G. Stone, 1854–1867.

SOUTH LAKE'S ICE CROPS

The Catskill Mountain House had its own icehouses to provide for its summer needs; additionally, it was generous in permitting locals to take cakes of ice from the lake for their own use. With the growing pollution of the Hudson River, as cities and villages disposed of their sewage into the river, concerns about health problems grew. Ice from purer sources such as private lakes, and even from as far away as Maine, was in demand. Between 1908 and 1916, Charles and George H. Beach & Company saw an additional source of income from their Catskill Mountain House property. They sought out an ice contractor dealing with metropolitan New York City, finding it in John D. Schoonmaker of Rondout, Ulster County.[1]

Each year from 1909 to 1916, the Beach company had its Catskill attorney, Frank Osborn, negotiate with Schoonmaker's Esopus Ice Company. This firm had ties with the Foster-Scott Ice Company, whose main office was at 332-334 West Eleventh Street, New York City. By 1913 Schoonmaker was serving as Foster-Scott's president.

Yearly options were taken up at $100, and that amount was applicable to the final bill for the winter season if Schoonmaker decided to harvest ice. For up to 5,000 tons, the going price was to be 8.5¢ per ton; for over 5,000 tons, 10¢. No trees were to be cut or interfered with, without the approval of the Mountain House superintendent, Mr. Sanford.

South Lake's Ice Crops

By February of 1910, Schoonmaker wrote that he had doubts about taking up the option for that season, because his icehouses were all filled. Each year thereafter Schoonmaker would be asked if he were interested in harvesting ice on South Lake, and each year he would send an option check of $100. The contracts did not vary much from year to year, but a new paragraph was added, allowing Charles and George H. Beach & Company, as well as other parties in the vicinity, to cut ice for their own use.

During the winter of 1913, George and his wife were in winter residence at the Williams Hotel in Daytona, Florida. From there Beach wrote to attorney Osborn: "I hear Mr. Schoonmaker is making preparation at Kaaterskill Station so that he can take ice as soon as of sufficient thickness. Perhaps he will pay for option from North Lake on same or lower terms. It would have to be loaded on sleigh or wagon and hauled one half mile. If ice is scarce, worth having." But the North Lake ice was not as attractive to the contractor. He preferred South Lake's ice because it was much nearer to the railroad tracks.

The South Lake boat house was owned by the Catskill Mountain House and used by its guests for recreational purposes. It was leased seasonally. Postcard, c. 1923.

February 1913 was a busy month. Schoonmaker paid $400 by the twelfth of the month, "having loaded up to last night 176 cars. If conditions on the river warrant our taking ice on North Lake we could take that also although very large tonnage on Kaaterskill (South) Lake." Local men had employment on the ice field all that February. By the eighteenth they had filled 373 railroad cars, all from Kaaterskill South Lake. The operations had to be suspended briefly until sufficient ice barges could be secured at Rondout. Schoonmaker offered to purchase a second cutting on South Lake at 5¢ per ton, rather than cut on North Lake. The offer was refused on the advice of Osborn, who was fearful it would set a precedent for a lower price the following winter. A second offer from Schoonmaker—to split the difference—also was refused.

The winter of 1912-1913 appears to have been the highlight of the Beach-Schoonmaker contractual relationship. Ice tally reports kept coming in as payments were made. By the end of February, the ice crews had cut and hauled to the railroad station 24,055 tons valued at 10¢ per ton, for a total value of $2,045.05. The Ulster and Delaware Railroad prepared weight statements for shipment via the Catskill and Tannersville and the Stony Clove lines.

Thereafter, Schoonmaker's interest seems to dwindle each succeeding year for a variety of reasons. In 1916 there was "too much snow." That appears to have been the last winter season that the Foster-Scott Ice Company (i.e., Schoonmaker) renewed its $100 option.

By March of 1919, the Beach women (Sarah, Ida, and Martha) had management control of the Mountain House property. They were unable to find a contractor as large as the Foster-Scott Ice Company, but they did manage to interest Arthur D. Palmer of Catskill in contracting for "not more than two hundred tons unless he shall elect to purchase more." Palmer had a retail ice company with routes in the village of Catskill. The Beaches apparently had filled the hotel's icehouses to capacity and were selling to Mr. Palmer out of their own supply. There is no indication Palmer actually harvested ice on either South or North Lake. He also paid $2.50 per ton for all ice remaining in the hotel's icehouses after September 1, 1919.

As industrial ice manufacturing grew in the 1920s, the lakes no longer held income potential from the sale of crops of ice, and no other such commercial contracts have been found in Beach family primary source papers.

South Lake's Ice Crops

Kaaterskill Clove ice formation labeled "The Ice Organ" in this stereoview by E. & H.T. Anthony, Winter in the Catskills series, 1870s.

![Fawn's Leap pencil drawing]

B.B.G. Stone, Fawn's Leap, *pencil drawing, September 26, 1866. Fawn's Leap, located about 100 yards upstream from Church's Ledge and Moore's Bridge, was one of the main scenic spots on the clove road before the state road was constructed. When talking about working in this area of the clove in a newspaper article, Stone not only gave the best date of the year in regard to catching the best light conditions, but the exact time of day as well.*

VI
THE CLOVE ROAD

The eastern escarpment of the Catskill Mountains bisects Greene County, which made travel between the county's Hudson River Valley communities and its mountaintop townships difficult. In the nineteenth century there was even a move by the more westerly mountaintop towns to form "their own geographic county."

The route through Kaaterskill Clove was one of the few "passes" leading from the valley to the mountaintop, but that winding dirt road was rutted in winter, muddy in spring, and dusty in summer. As the automobile became a daily necessity, the patience of residents grew thin. The political process called for state action.

From the sketchbooks of B.B.G. Stone, 1854–1867.

Traveling Kaaterskill Clove

T. Addison Richards (1820-1900) described walking along the bed of Kaaterskill Creek, rather than on the frequented path. To do so, however, meant making a number of detours to see the magnificent pass, and risking danger to life and limb for a mile-and-a-half until a rickety wooden bridge was reached (which is now known as Moore's, but which Richards identified only as "at the High Rocks").

Van Loan's *Catskill Mountain Guide*, which was first made available to the public in 1876, provides a detailed description of a recommended "Ride Around the Clove." This entailed first going down the Beach private toll road with the Mountain House only visible on the long, level approach. Various sections of this mountain road carried such names as Featherbed Hill, Short Level and Cape Horn. The latter is a steep, half-circle curve at the end of Short Level.

The Rip Van Winkle House was then a stopping-off place much used by hikers and riders. The curious could see the flat rock marked "Rip's Rock," the purported scene of Rip's long sleep.

Van Loan's circuit continued on the toll road and then along the base of South Mountain until one met the clove road. Proceeding west one gained a vista of Palenville Overlook and, after passing the studio of artist George Hall, came to Burger's Hotel, a rest stop for man, horse and oxen.

As Van Loan pointed out, some spots, like Artist's Grotto and LaBelle Falls, required leaving the main road. Moving onward, mention was made of the tollgate and two areas prone to landslides. Looking northward along the base of South Mountain gave a view of a wild-looking ravine called the Gulf.

Van Loan was acquainted with conservationist E. T. Mason who had a rustic summer cottage along this area of the clove. Next came the Chasm, after which one crossed a stream that Van Loan did not identify, but which is located at Moore's

Toll booth on the old clove road. The road was narrow, muddy at times, extremely difficult to maintain, frequently closed in winter for short periods of time, and more suitable for horses, carriages, and wagons than automobiles. Postcard, c. 1908.

Bridge. Church's Ledge and Profile Rock are located here. The old road—the main road in Van Loan's time—brought one past Hillyer's Ravine and to Fawn's Leap.

In succession came Wild Cat Ravine, the ruins of Brockett's in the Clove (an inn once frequented by many artists), the ruins of East Hunter village and the tannery, and Buttermilk Falls.

Near the Lake Creek bridge was a path to Bastion Falls and Kaaterskill Falls. A path leading from the left of this bridge provided an opportunity to see Triton Cave, Shelving Rock and the Five Cascades, and led on to the base of Haines Falls. Van Loan noted that the latter was accessed more easily by descending the stairs at the falls.

Side paths for the more venturesome produced views not frequently seen by travelers in those days.

Moore's Bridge (sometimes spelled More's Bridge) spans the Kaaterskill Creek at Church's Ledge. Today this is a popular recreation area for hikers. The bridge is thought to be named for artist Charles Herbert Moore, who resided on a hillside farm just north of today's Rip Van Winkle Bridge. Photograph, 1870s.

The old stagecoach road at Palenville made use of planking over difficult terrain. Photograph, 1890s.

From the sketchbooks of B.B.G. Stone, 1854–1867.

THE CLOVE RACE THAT FIZZLED OUT

It was thought to be one of the best promotional ideas in a century—a touring car contest that would bring to Greene County over 1,000 participants and more than 20,000 spectators. It would be better even than the "Montauk Light or Bust" run on Long Island.

The early twentieth century saw the promotion of endurance runs by competing motorists; it was a sport distinct from track-car racing. Motorists (all men in those years) were ever quick to boast of the power of their new, four-wheeled acquisitions and the hills they climbed without trouble. Throughout the United States similar contests attracted wide attention. Senator W.J. Morgan was one of the leading promoters. Could Senator Morgan be enlisted to help promote a Greene County automobile run up Kaaterskill Clove, a route of major challenge and rated as second in difficulty in the Northeast only to Mount Washington?

Off went a petition to Senator Morgan, signed by a number of Greene County men. And back came the reply that the senator indeed would consider promoting such a "tour and hill climb" in July 1910. On June 11, a Saturday afternoon, the Morgan party left New York City with two Pathfinder cars, an Auburn and a Westcott. Included, in addition to Senator Morgan, were photographers and newspaper reporters who would all help decide about the proposed clove run. It would be a weekend in the country; they would all return to the city on Monday.

The Clove Race that Fizzled Out

Moore's Bridge on the Kaaterskill was subject to washouts from torrential downpours. A team of oxen hauling quarry slate once broke through the wooden span. Photograph, c. 1885.

THE CLOVE ROAD

The Palenville Hotel was a stop-off for man and beast before ascending the clove road. There were other, earlier hotels on this site, some of which burned.

Using the Grant house (Jefferson Heights, Catskill) as headquarters, Senator Morgan and his entourage announced the makeup of the inspection party on June 11. In addition to Catskill men such as Percival G. Doty, Dr. Heisinger of Palenville would assemble several cars at that hamlet. Down from Tannersville and Haines Falls would come Roger Voss and Frank Lawn, representing the mountaintop.

Close inspection of the clove road, especially the steep hill between the Lake Creek bridge and Haines Falls, followed and the route passed inspection. Plans for the race moved ahead rapidly, and the weekend of July 16-18 was found to be acceptable to

The Clove Race that Fizzled Out

all. The American Automobile Association was asked to sanction the event. The Westchester Bankers Association, however, issued a warning to their members to be very cautious because people were becoming automobile crazy. At its Briarcliff Hotel meeting, the association urged bank staff to look carefully into loan applications for the purchase of cars by means of discounted promissory notes.

The Greene County newspapers now labeled the planned event as an International Hill Climb or Motor Contest, and the local committee headed by Percival Doty organized under the name of the Motor Car Association. The three-day event called for a Saturday "Reliability Run" to weed out problem cars, a Sunday of touring the northern Catskills and resting, while Monday was reserved for the "Official Climb." Rules were established, including one requiring all participants taking part in the endurance run to use the same gear ratio in the climb up the final steep hill as in the run itself. Racing cars would be disallowed.

The prizes were prestige items, not cash. Specially designed bronze plaque shields would be affixed to the winners' cars. The Greene County Sheriff's Department—Abram Post and his deputies—were asked to supervise the anticipated, very heavy influx of entrants and spectators, and to guarantee safety and noninterference with the climb. Enthusiasm continued to grow. Hotel and boardinghouse proprietors saw it as a "full house" deal. Other businessmen were convinced the dollars would flow from a free-spending crowd.

As an added inducement to attract more entrants, other than the eight categories of gasoline-powered cars costing from $800 to $4,000 and more, amateur car owners from Catskill or "a radius of fifteen miles of Kaaterskill Clove Mountain" could compete in a special category. For all entrants the fee was $10 and required filling out an application form.

Automobile owners could be seen on the old clove road the next few weeks, giving special attention to the stretch starting at the Lake Creek bridge and ending at Haines Falls House.

The weekend came and went without a race; the newspapers offered no explanation.[1] To this day historians are still puzzled. Was it for lack of entrants? Was the clove road too dangerous? Was there a competing event? What is known, however, is that one of the best Greene County promotional events never occurred, and within a few years the state began a major reconstruction of the clove road.

From the sketchbooks of B.B.G. Stone, 1854–1867.

"Jacob's Ladder" or the "Rip Van Winkle Trail"?

By 1910 the automobile was no longer considered a pleasure vehicle for "better weather" use, to be stored on blocks over the winter months; it had become a primary source of transportation, both commercial and private. With its increased use came the demand for improved roads. "Good Roads" associations and chambers of commerce were at the forefront of lobbying for better roads, as were the newspapers. Gradually the New York State Legislature absorbed the message that good roads were not primarily a county and town responsibility. Financial assistance came in the form of two bond acts. In 1915 the large sum of $565,000 was made available from the state for Greene County road improvements, with the restriction that two-fifths of that sum had to be expended on state highways in the county.

Because of its importance as a main conduit between the valley and the mountaintop, the clove road got the lion's share of the appropriation. Justification for this was based on the number of reported vehicle accidents in 1914, some with injuries from crashing into the gorge. (In 1920 the International Film Company shot a scene in the clove of an automobile going over a cliff.) The Greene County weekly newspapers supported improvement of the clove road with printed statements:

"Jacob's Ladder" or the "Rip Van Winkle Trail"?

The improved state highway known as the Rip Van Winkle Trail, 1920s. Note the gravel base surface of that period.

THE CLOVE ROAD

A precursor of the convenience store, Rip's Lookout on the Rip Van Winkle Trail was a refreshment stand and gasoline station. The building is now gone, replaced by a parking lot that serves hikers headed to Bastion Falls on Horseshoe Curve and Kaaterskill Falls. Postcard, 1930s.

"Weekly crews are constantly in demand all summer and in winter the old road is barely passable at the best and part of the time not at all."

At first no road-building construction firm was interested in taking on the four-mile stretch between Palenville and Haines Falls. It was fraught with construction difficulties and considered, at best, a break-even contract at the state-suggested estimate of $190,000.

The idea of using convict labor for the clove road first came from Greene County Clerk George B. VanValkenburgh. In 1913 he had secured the interest of Assemblyman J. Lewis Petrie in introducing a bill in the state legislature authorizing the use of convict labor. The following year Assemblyman George H. Chase completed the process. The final bill restricted the stretch of road to an 8 percent grade.

"Jacob's Ladder" or the "Rip Van Winkle Trail"?

Moving rapidly in the convict labor road-building experiment, contracts were soon signed for summer barracks, a mess hall, laundry, and shower facilities. In the meantime convicts interested in participating were screened in the state prisons.

It was one of those experiments with prison labor that continue to pop up at intervals. The state today has forestry camps, which provide less arduous work. At best the VanValkenburgh idea was only a partial success, since the terrain is among the most difficult for unskilled labor. Also affecting the experiment was the outbreak of World War I in Europe. With a ready market for America's iron, steel, and other manufactured goods, the labor market became very tight and fewer men entered the prison population, especially after the United States declared war in 1917.

By the time the peace process was underway, state engineers were once again looking to complete the state road through the clove. Their new cost estimate was now $169,941.50. The state advertised for bids, but was disappointed when it received none by the October 20, 1920, deadline. A second attempt finally captured the inter-

The scenic Horseshoe Curve on the Rip Van Winkle Trail. Postcard, 1930s.

205

Even after the state rebuilt the clove road, washouts were a frequent problem. This one in 1936 was especially serious and required the closing of the highway until repairs could be made.

est of Ward and Tully, of Brooklyn, and the State Highway Department lost no time in awarding the clove road contract for their bid of $174,091.50. State specifications included a gravel wearing course to provide better traction to prevent vehicle slippage in the winter months.

At the meeting of the Greene County Board of Supervisors on April 14, 1919, speakers had urged the board to appropriate $20,629.65 as the county share to complete Kaaterskill Clove State Highway Project No. 5588. The state was providing an additional $58,715.17. By vote of the supervisors, twenty coupon bonds with a face value of $1,000 each were issued, paying 5 percent interest.

On a Tuesday in late November 1921, County Engineer George H. Penfield and a representative of the State Highway Department could be seen traveling over the

"Jacob's Ladder" or the "Rip Van Winkle Trail"?

A cave-in on the Rip Van Winkle Trail in 1936. A truck blocks the roadway, preventing public use.

newly completed clove road, giving it a final inspection before "throwing the road open for use." The subbase, which was covered with gravel, was thought to provide a good traction surface. A top dressing was yet to be done because they were waiting for funds to be appropriated. The local newspapers were happy, claiming that "The use of the highway will be a great convenience to the mountaineers who can now come to Catskill without going by way of East Windham which has been in rather bad shape for winter travel."

The new clove road was only partially successful, however, as was noted by the Catskill Recorder in late March of 1922, when it referred to the dangerous spring conditions of the new road, "rutted with automobile tracks deep in the ice. Along the Clove have occurred several landslides, the cause being the spring thaw. Fortunately the road base itself is as solid as a rock."[1]

There was much talk of a summer 1922 clove road celebration, with schoolchildren performing in pageants and automobiles coming from all parts of the county, but there is no evidence that such a celebration occurred.

The weekly *Examiner* now challenged its readers to come up with an appropriate name for the new clove road. Both serious and humorous suggestions were received. J.F. Back of Onteora Park, Tannersville, favored the name "Jacob's Ladder." His letter read:

Dear Editor:

Of late discussion for an appropriate road name, many suggestions unworthy. Facts:

1. The *Examiner* refers to Top of Mountain as a place of paradise. We call it God's own Country. Our summer cousins call it the promised land. We must all agree this must be Heaven and that the new road leads to Heaven.
2. Suffering humanity who have had to travel the new road leading to the Catskills heard rumors of this new "Gateway to the Catskills"
3. The work on the road which is now being pushed is the result of Assemblyman Jacobs.
4. In other words what we require is from the above, a name for Jacob's road to Heaven. Somehow we look to the Scriptures and think of that other wonderful dream and lo—we have found it. What else could it be but "Jacob's Ladder?" I therefore suggest that future generations make arrangements for one grand pageant to be held at the completion and that all the angels bring forth each his "mountain dew" and christen the road "Jacob's Ladder."

"Jacob's Ladder" or the "Rip Van Winkle Trail"?

But "Jacob's Ladder" it was not to be, "Rip Van Winkle" being too strong a competitor. The improved roadway became the Rip Van Winkle Trail.

Private entrepreneurs were quick to take advantage of the new state highway. In March 1922 Joseph J. Hoy of Catskill announced he would inaugurate a freight line between Catskill and Hunter using a five-ton truck. There would be frequent stops along the route, and his customers could be assured that his rates would save them at least 25 percent on freight costs. William Garrison of Palenville ordered two, thirty-passenger buses from the Amos Post Agency, with delivery scheduled for April 15. His intent was to operate a bus line between Catskill Point and Tannersville, "passing the grandest scenery on earth."

This promotional booklet view, c. 1930, depicts the Hotel Palenville, which boasted hot and cold running water in each room and electric lights. Note the winding clove road with the legend "3 1/2 M to Haines Falls."

From the sketchbooks of B.B.G. Stone, 1854–1867.

EPILOGUE: THOMAS COLE, CEDAR GROVE, AND KAATERSKILL CLOVE

The northern Catskills stand out boldly against the skyline when viewed from the west piazza of Cedar Grove, Thomas Cole's village of Catskill home. The various peaks and cloves, including Kaaterskill Clove, are identified on the viewshed map stand. Also there are three lines from Cole's 1836 poem, *The Wild:*

> Friend of my heart, lovers of nature's work
> Let me transport you to those wild blue mountains
> That rear their summits near the Hudson's waves.[1]

From his first sketching trip to the northern Catskills in 1825 to the end of his lifetime, Cole maintained a paramount interest in this expanse of Catskill Mountains scenery. The restored Cedar Grove, rated a National Historic Landmark by the state and federal governments as a site of exceptional cultural importance, is designed to focus visitor attention on the importance of Thomas Cole in the history of American art and the early environmental movement, and his well-merited place in the heritage of the nation.

Thomas Cole, Cedar Grove, and Kaaterskill Clove

National and international interest continues to grow as the Hudson River School of Landscape Painting—and Thomas Cole's part in its founding—attracts more devotees with each new generation. There have been a number of new books in recent decades, while special or permanent museum exhibitions are an important part of educational efforts.

Directly across the Hudson River from Cedar Grove is Olana, the creation of Frederic E. Church. For more than two years Church was a student of Cole's and benefited from his shared professional experience. After Cole's death, Church remained a lifelong friend of Cole's widow and children.

There is much public rejoicing that Thomas Cole's Cedar Grove finally has reached "safe harbor" after close calls with destruction. Plans for the western approach to the Rip Van Winkle Bridge in the early 1930s would have condemned the artist's home and studio were it not for public outcry and family support. The approach was diverted instead to the northern edge of the village of Catskill.

In the 1960s, owner Edith Cole Hill Silberstein sought to preserve for the public benefit this National Historic Landmark site and much of its art holdings, which included some of those of her great-grandfather, Thomas Cole. Silberstein spoke of that effort in an August 2003 letter:

> From its inception in 1815 Cedar Grove was the home of members of the Thomson, Bartow and Cole families and their descendents. I inherited the estate from my aunt, Florence Cole Vincent, upon her death in 1961, and was the last family member to own and occupy the property.
>
> Florence Vincent had lived in the house all her life and lovingly preserved it and tended the abundant flower gardens and the outbuildings. She wanted it to continue as a haven for family members and a home we could all enjoy, which it was until 1979 when it became the property of The Catskill Center for Conservation and Development.
>
> Beginning in 1962, I endeavored to find purchasers for Cedar Grove. I started with the State of New York. Dr. Albert Corey of the Education Department was very interested, and with the help of Assemblyman Larry Lane a Bill was presented to the Legislature for acquisition. The property, with the exception of the old studio at the west end of the driveway, which I wanted to make into a summer home for my family, was offered to the State for a very low price including the remaining Cole paintings. This was a small amount as I was mainly interested in the preservation of the estate and paintings and the formation of a museum open to the public. However, the State Budget Director, Mr. Hurd turned down the offer due to heavy expenses and very tight budget that year, and the Bill was not presented to Governor Rockefeller for signature.
>
> I started to look elsewhere. There were many years of consultations with the National Trust, National Park Service, artists' groups and collectors of art.
>
> In 1979 The Catskill Center purchased the property to hold until a suitable owner could be found. They sold Cedar Grove in 1982 to a group of two owners of art galleries and two collectors. They formed The Thomas Cole Foundation. The house was open to the public as a

EPILOGUE

museum for some years, but eventually two of the members dropped out of the Foundation, and it became difficult for the remaining ones to continue.

Meanwhile in Washington in 1994 interested members of Congress presented a Bill for acquisition of the property by the Federal Government, Cedar Grove to be part of the National Park Service. The Bill was passed by the House of Representatives but the Senate lacked sufficient votes despite the interest of Senator Moynihan, and it was defeated.

Raymond Beecher, President and later Chairman of the Board of the Greene County Historical Society, had been interested in Cedar Grove for many years. He paid us frequent visits and in 1997 the Society purchased the property from Ira Spanierman of the Spanierman Galleries in New York City, who was in control of the remains of the Foundation. In November

Thomas Cole's Cedar Grove is located just south of the Rip Van Winkle Bridge. The main house shown here dates from 1815; the separate studio building was constructed in 1839. Both have been restored and opened to the public as a National Historic Landmark affiliated with the National Park Service. Photograph, September 1991.

1998, Cedar Grove became the property of the Greene County Historical Society. My family and I rejoiced. The long struggle was over.[2]

Despite Thomas Cole's travels abroad and in this country, above all he loved Cedar Grove. His home and family were very dear to him, as were the Catskill Mountains, whose beauty and serenity were a great source of inspiration.

And now the magnificent restoration of Cedar Grove is a fitting tribute to one of America's great artists!"

Edith Cole Silberstein
Great-granddaughter of Thomas Cole and Maria Bartow Cole

In July of 2001, a celebration of the bicentennial of Thomas Cole's birth was held at Cedar Grove with over 1,500 persons in attendance. There was much praise for the superb restoration work performed by the craftsmen of Catskill's Dimensions North. It was a time to appreciate the interest and financial support that had come from hundreds of individuals and corporate bodies: the purchase price had come from the Raymond Beecher Trust, supplemented by Helen McCord's gift of her Spring Street house, on land that was once part of the Cedar Grove orchard; the New York State Bond Act of 1996 provided some exterior restoration funds as administered by the department of Parks, Recreation and Historic Preservation; the paint and related materials were donated by Benjamin Moore & Company, a firm that continues to maintain a strong interest in the site. The Catskill Center for Conservation and Development is to be commended for its long-term interest in Cedar Grove. Then Executive Director Darlene Downing and her staff gave top priority to the New York State Bond Act grant application, which was almost at deadline.

Today, as a result of a bill sponsored by Congressman John E. Sweeney and Senator Daniel P. Moynihan, Thomas Cole's Cedar Grove is designated an "Affiliated Site" of the National Park Service. Cedar Grove remains locally owned and operated, but the federal agency provides a wealth of technical assistance, including a Department of the Interior General Management Plan as developed by Dr. James O'Connell and assistants. Save America's Treasures and the Athens Generating Mitigation Fund have financed the restoration of the 1839 Cole studio.

Finally the Artists' Trail, which will lead from the Hudson Valley into the northern Catskills via Kaaterskill Clove, will provide an additional aspect to public education about the Hudson River School of Landscape Painting. As the twenty-first century sees Thomas Cole and the sites closely connected with him deeply enshrined in the annals of American art, Kaaterskill Clove is a fundamental part.

ABOUT THE AUTHOR

Raymond Beecher was born in New York City in 1917 and is a 14th-generation descendent of George Baxter, English secretary to Peter Stuyvesant, the Dutch colonial governor of New Amsterdam. His family moved upriver to Greene County in 1927.

Mr. Beecher earned his bachelor's degree from Hartwick College and his master's degree from Boston University. During World War II he served in both the Asiatic-Pacific and European theaters of operation.

The Greene County Legislature has appointed Raymond Beecher as the county's official historian since 1993. He also serves as volunteer librarian for the Vedder Research Library, and has served as president and as chairman of the board of the Greene County Historical Society, an organization to which he has belonged for more than fifty years. Mr. Beecher provided the funds to purchase and begin the restoration process that saved Thomas Cole's Cedar Grove estate from the wrecking ball, and he initiated the Greene County Historical Sites Register. In recognition of his distinguished career, he was awarded a Doctor of Humane Letters by Hartwick College.

Raymond Beecher is the author of *Under Three Flags*; *Out to Greenville*; *Around Greene County and the Catskills* (with Harvey Durham); numerous magazine articles and a weekly newspaper column on local history called "Greene Gleanings." He is the editor of *Letters from a Revolution*.

Mr. Beecher lives in Coxsackie on the west bank of the Hudson River in the home he shared with his wife of fifty years, Catharine Shaffer Beecher.

END NOTES

Prologue

1. Jessie Van Vechten Vedder long maintained the local Anglo-Dutch tradition that Jacob Katz provided the name. *See* Vedder, *Historic Catskill*, page 2. Shirley Dunn, a fine scholar and researcher, provides the theory in her 1994 book, *The Mohicans and Their Land* (page 245), that the name is derived from an Anglo-Dutch corruption of Kaankat, the name of a local Indian who signed a Catskill deed in 1649. He was possibly the same person the Mohicans called Cat, the first Mohican mentioned by name in Dutch records (1626), which identify him as a "captain of the Mohicans."

2. *Highway Map and Scenic Tours of Greene County, New York*, 1999, by Gary R. Harvey and Thomas Colucci.

3. The Revolutionary War-period British and Indian raids are a part of the history of the town of Catskill. *See* J. Van Vechten Vedder, *History of Greene County, 1651-1800* for the Abeel raid (page 63) and the Strope raid (page 33) at Round Top (the small mountain called *Wa-wan-te-kook*). See also J. Van Vechten Vedder, *Historic Catskill*, 17, 91. In Raymond Beecher, *Letters from a Revolution*, there is a letter dated 24 May 1781 from Captain Philip Conine Jr. to Leonard Bronck at Coxsackie detailing scouting expeditions against British and Indian raiding parties.

4. From an undated typescript article by George H. Peters written to support state and national listing on the Natural Register. This botanical information helped secure national recognition for Kaaterskill Clove.

I Legend and Lore

Rip Van Winkle

1. Various articles about the literary career of Washington Irving suggest he heard of such "long sleeps" folklore while serving in the diplomatic service abroad. Legends of long sleeps date back to ancient times, but most have Central European roots.

2. Richard S. Barrett, booklet entitled *The Land of Rip Van Winkle*, for Catskill Chamber of Commerce.

3. Letters and other related material are to be found in the Mabel Parker Smith Memorial Collection, Vedder Research Library.

4. *The Autobiography of Joseph Jefferson* (Harvard University Press, 1964), 170.

5. Ibid., 336.

6. Mabel Parker Smith and Maxim Karolik correspondence, Vedder Research Library.

II The Clove in American Art

Nineteenth-Century Artists in the Clove: The Hudson River School

1. As a young adult Luman Reed (1787-1836) resided in the village of Coxsackie, Greene County. Subsequently he joined relatives in New York City. *See* Raymond Beecher, "Luman Reed—He Made American Artists the Fashion," *Greene County Historical Journal*, summer 1978.

2. See Matthew Baigell, *Thomas Cole* (New York: Watson-Guptil Publications, 1991). Publishers have produced a number of volumes since World War II pertaining to the Hudson River School of Art. Elwood Parry's volume being the most comprehensive as it relates to Thomas Cole. Others have concentrated on individual artists or on certain themes. Roland Van Zandt's *The Catskill Mountain House* (Black Dome Press, 1991) has an excellent overview in Chapter Seven, "The Hudson River School of Painting."

Kindred Spirits

1. Ella M. Foshay and Barbara Novak, *Intimate Friends* (The New-York Historical Society, 2000).

2. Letters and newspapers clippings relating to this controversy are to be found in the Mabel Parker Smith Memorial Collection, Vedder Research Library, the gift of Barbara Smith Rivette.

Poor Man's Art

1. Richard Crouse, *Mr. Currier and Mr. Ives* (Garden City Publishing Company, 1936).

2. R.T. Haines Halsey, *Pictures of Early New York on Dark Blue Staffordshire Pottery* (Dover Publication, 1974), 43, 47. Ellouise Larsen, *American Historical Views on Staffordshire China* (Dover Publication, 1975).

3. Roland Van Zandt, *The Catskill Mountain House*, op. cit., 59.

Stereoscopic Views

1. Ripley and Dana, eds., *The American Cyclopaedia* (New York: Appleton's, 1881).

2. This S. Root is thought to be Stephen Root, a tanner from Catskill.

END NOTES

E.T. Mason, Patron Saint of Kaaterskill Clove

1. R. Lionel DeLisser, *Picturesque Catskills, Greene County* (North Hampton, Mass.: Picturesque Publishing Co., 1894), 40. B.B.G. Stone's drawings—signed with an S superimposed over a T— are to be found in this volume, especially in the Kaaterskill Clove section.

B.B.G. Stone, Second Generation of the Hudson River School

1. In its January 1978 issue of its quarterly magazine, the New-York Historical Society published Catherine Campbell's short biography of Benjamin Bellows Grant Stone under the title, "A Forgotten American Artist." Campbell had made use of the Vedder Research Library holdings.

2. Stone had a local following, with visitors frequently calling at his rented carriage house studio off Orange Street (now Prospect Avenue). The weekly newspaper *Catskill Examiner* often printed his prose. The quoted sections are either from Stone's diaries or the *Examiner*.

The Palenville Art Colony

1. Roland Van Zandt, *The Catskill Mountain House*, op. cit., 175-78, 182, 183, 223.

2. R. Lionel DeLisser, *Picturesque Catskills, Greene County*; op. cit. There also is a photo on page 35 of Hall working at his easel in his studio.

Walton Van Loan

1. Journal, Vedder Research Library, Van Loan folder.

2. Raymond Beecher, "JoeWaltz—Between Murders He Wrote Poetry," *Greene County Historical Journal*, spring and summer 1978.

3. After Van Loan's death these copyrights were found tied up in a small bundle with the label "For Theodore Cole." The Coles of Cedar Grove, Catskill, were cousins of Walton Van Loan via the Thomson lineage. The copyrights were given to the Vedder Research Library, the gift of Thomas and Maria Cole's great-granddaughter, Edith Cole Silberstein.

➤ III Literary Sketches

European Travel Writers

1. Roger Haydon, in *Upstate Travels: British Views of Nineteenth-Century New York* (Syracuse University Press, 1982), has compiled a reference list of over seventy such travel writers.

American Writers—Amateur and Professional

1. Frank Racette, a Thomas Cole's Cedar Grove Board of Advisors member, acquired this 1825 issue of the *Rhode Island American* and presented it to Cedar Grove. Until Racette's find, this account was virtually unknown to Catskill Mountain authors.

➤ IV Grand Hotels and Private Parks

1. Hotel brochures, "free upon request," were often saved by hotel guests, and several have been donated to the Vedder Research Library. More elaborate booklets could be purchased at the hotel's lobby newsstands.

2. Susan Eltinge, *Highlights of Twilight History* (privately published pamphlet, 1971).

The Laurel House

1. The relationships between the Beach family of the Catskill Mountain House and the Schutt family of the Laurel House were close, unlike the rivalry between the Beaches and the Hardings of Hotel Kaaterskill. There were marriages between the Beaches, Gardiners and the Schutts, and some of the Schutt offspring secured summertime employment at the Mountain House.

Guests at the Mountain House, 1922

1. The promotional booklet circa 1922 reflects the more active management style of John K. Van Wagonen. Money had been procured in one way or another to modernize the hotel, especially its plumbing. The affluent 1920s made the summer vacation a part of almost everyone's lifestyle.

The Mountain House for Sale

1. The Catskill law firm of Osborn, Bloodgood, Wilbur and Fray, which provided legal services to many affluent families, gradually took in new partners as the older ones retired from active practice. At the time of the sale of the Main Street, Catskill, building of the Cooperative Insurance Company to the Bank of Greene County, the successor law firm of Bagley, Pulver, Stiefel and Winans moved to new offices in the old Gaylord Opera House, across the street from the county courthouse. In the process of moving, the law firm made decades of legal folders available to the Greene County Historical Society's Vedder Research Library. The author, assisted by Valentine Kriele, then-president of the historical society, moved three station wagon loads of records for screening for historical use. The Beach family records were among those holdings. The records were not complete, but proved to be informative about the final years of the famed hotel while under Beach–Van Wagonen control.

Mountain House Finale

1. The saga of Milo Claude Moseman's efforts to preserve at least the main, original section of the Catskill Mountain House is a tragedy of the times. Even with the best of intentions there was little money to make essential repairs while the nation suffered through the great economic depression of the 1930s and World War II. Perhaps fate was kind to Moseman; he did not live to see the Mountain House burned.

Homes near to Nature

1. Summer life in Twilight Park during the period just prior to World War I is well reflected in Edward F. Bigelow's article. Although severely buffeted by the economic depression of the 1930s, Twilight Park, which eventually absorbed Santa Cruz Park, managed to survive as an entity. Today it is sometimes referred to as "existing in its own world," set apart from the normal everyday lifestyle on the mountaintop. Haines Falls plunges down a rock face on privately owned, Twilight Park land, separating Twilight Park from Route 23A and helping isolate the community.

❧V Harvesting the Clove's Resources

Industry in the Clove

1. The late Esther Haines Dunn was very knowledgeable about the top of the clove. Over the years she contributed articles for the Greene County Historical Society's *Journal*, including "A Certain Small House," "Harry Fenn, Illustrator," and "Saw Mills on a Mountain Top." In conversations either at her family's summer house, where my wife and I were invited for tea, or at my home, Esther usually had a story or two to tell about "Christian Charley."

Logging the Pine Orchard

1. The legal papers relating to the Pine Orchard logging operation are also part of the Chadderdon, Pulver, Stiefel, and Winans Collection, now at the Vedder Research Library. From a conservation standpoint, every precaution was taken to do as little damage to the environment and scenery as possible.

South Lake's Ice Crops

1. Unlike the timber harvesting of first-growth trees, the Beach family saw ice harvesting as a yearly, renewable crop, an enterprise that did little or no environmental damage. The availability of rail connections through the Stony Clove and down to Kingston made the South Lake ice competitive in price with ice harvested on the Hudson River. (The ice was never transported over the Otis or the Catskill Mountain Railroad, which were strictly "fair weather" railways.)

❧VI The Clove Road

The Clove Race That Fizzled Out

1. Articles of varying length about the proposed "Haines Falls or Bust" race appear in several issues of the *Catskill Examiner*, but research has yet to find any mention of the race's failure to run.
One can only conjecture.

"Jacob's Ladder" or the "Rip Van Winkle Trail"?

1. The well-traveled Rip Van Winkle Trail still causes headaches for highway district engineers: the terrain on the slopes above the creek is subject to landslides; there are no passing lanes; parking is very limited except for two small lots (one official and one unofficial). Scenic pollution is always a concern. Local preservationists were able to convince the state to construct a stone retaining wall above Moore's Bridge instead of a less expensive metal and concrete wall. Drivers must be alert to the road's twists and turns. To fully enjoy the beauties of the clove, the best advice is to let someone else do the driving!

❧Epilogue

1. It was Sybil Tannenbaum of the Cedar Grove Board of Governors who championed the use of these lines. Countless visitors read them as they gaze on the northern Catskills.

2. Thomas Cole's Cedar Grove National Historic Landmark is a prime example of a successful "grass roots" preservation effort that seemingly was slated for failure. Edith Cole Silberstein continues to maintain contact by letter and telephone from Vero Beach, Florida.

ADDITIONAL READING

Avery, Kevin J., and Franklin Kelly. *Hudson River School Visions:* The Landscapes of Sanford R. Gifford. New York: The Metropolitan Museum of Art, 2003.

Baigell, Matthew. *Thomas Cole.* New York: Watson-Guptil, 1981.

Beers, J.B., ed. *History of Greene County.* New York: J.B. Beers & Co., 1884.

Bryant, William C., ed. *Picturesque America.* New York: Appleton, 1872-74.

DeLisser, R. Lionel. *Picturesque Catskills: Greene County.* Northampton, Mass.: Picturesque Publishing Co., 1894.

Doeffinger, Derek, and Keith Boas. *Waterfalls of the Adirondacks and Catskills.* Ithaca, N.Y.: McBooks Press, 2000.

Driscoll, John. *All That Is Glorious around Us: Paintings from the Hudson River School.* Ithaca, N.Y.: Cornell University Press, 1997.

Dumond, Frank L. *Tall Tales of the Catskills.* New York: Atheneum, 1968.

Evers, Alf. *The Catskills: From Wilderness to Woodstock.* Garden City, N.Y.: Doubleday & Co., 1972.

Foshay, Ella M. *Mr. Luman's Picture Gallery.* New York: Harry N. Abrams, 1990.

Foshay, Ella M., and Barbara Novak. *Intimate Friends: Thomas Cole, Asher B. Durand, William Cullen Bryant.* New York: New-York Historical Society, 2000.

Helmer, William F. *Rip Van Winkle Railroads.* 1970. Reprint, Hensonville, N.Y.: Black Dome Press Corp., 1999.

Horne, Field. *The Greene County Catskills: A History.* Hensonville, N.Y.: Black Dome Press Corp., 1994.

Howat, John K. *The Hudson River and Its Painters.* New York: Penguin Books, 1978.

Longstreth, T. Morris. *The Catskills.* 1918. Reprint, Hensonville, N.Y.: Black Dome Press Corp., 2003.

Mack, Arthur C. *Enjoying the Catskills.* New York: Funk & Wagnalls, 1950.

Mountain Top Historical Society. *Kaaterskill: From the Catskill Mountain House to the Hudson River School.* Hensonville, N.Y.: Black Dome Press Corp., 1993.

Myers, Kenneth. *The Catskills: Painters, Writers, and Tourists in the Mountains, 1820-1895.* Yonkers, N.Y.: Hudson River Museum, 1987.

Noble, Louis Legrand. *The Life and Works of Thomas Cole.* 1964. Reprint, Hensonville, N.Y.: Black Dome Press Corp., 1997.

Posselt, Eric. *The Rip Van Winkle Trail: A Guide to the Catskills.* Haines Falls, N.Y.: Arrowhead Press, 1952.

Rockwell, Rev. Charles. *The Catskill Mountains and the Region Around.* 1867. Reprint, Saugerties, N.Y.: Hope Farm Press, 1973.

Searing, Anna E. *The Land of Rip Van Winkle.* New York: G.P. Putnam's, 1884.

Siegel, Nancy. *Along the Juniata: Thomas Cole and the Dissemination of American Landscape Imagery.* Huntington, Penn.: Juniata College Museum of Art, 2003.

Van Loan, Walton. *Catskill Mountain Guide.* 1879. Reprint, Astoria, N.Y.: J.C. & A.L. Fawcett, Inc., n.d.

Van Zandt, Roland. *The Catskill Mountain House.* 1966. Reprint, Hensonville, N.Y.: Black Dome Press Corp., 1993.

Vedder, Jessie Van Vechten. *Historic Catskill.* 1922. Reprint, Astoria, N.Y.: J.C. & A.L. Fawcett, Inc., n.d.

———. *History of Greene County, 1651-1800.* Catskill, N.Y.: Examiner Press, 1927.

Yager, Bert D. *The Hudson River School: American Landscape Artists.* TODRI Book Publishers, 1999.

INDEX

A

African-Americans, 179
Allen's Photographic Gallery, 61
Alligator Rock (Whale Rock), 143
American Art Union, 54
Anderle, Donald, 50-51
Anthony, E. & H.T., 59, 60-61, 78, 86, 94, 104, 123, 131, 191
Appleton's General Guide to the United States and Canada, 107
Arnat, 71
Artist's Grotto, 195
Artists' Rock, 97
Artists' Trail, 35, 213
Atlantic Monthly, 60

B

Back, J.F., 208
Bailey, Banks and Biddle, 132
Barkley, Belle and Beulah, 157
Bartlett, William H., 54, 75, 99
Bastion Falls, 46, 60, 196
Beach, Charles (great-nephew), 154
Beach, Charles (son of Charles L.), 182-187
Beach, Charles L., 88, 94, 114, 156, 182, 183
Beach, George H., 146, 182-187
Beach, Ida Gardiner (Mrs. George H.), 88, 146, 147-153, 190
Beach, Louis (great-nephew), 154
Beach, Martha Congdon (Mrs. Charles), 146, 190
Beach, Sarah Avery, 82, 146, 147-153, 182-186, 190
Beach View (*see* Catskill Mountain House)
Beachview Post Office, 145
Bears Den, 85, 121
Beecher Trust, 213
Benjamin Moore & Company, 213
Bennett, William J., 54
Berger, Max, 93
Bigelow, Edward F., 166
Bigelow family, 134
boardinghouses (Haines family), 178
botany, 15
Boulder Rock (South Mountain), 131
Boutelle, DeWitt C., 45
Brockett's in the Clove, 43-44, 47, 63, 66, 71, 76, 196
Bronck Homestead, 164
Browere, Albertus del Orient, 29
Brownscombe, Jennie, 78-79
Bryant, William C., 48, 50-51, 56, 75, 105
Buckingham, James S., 94-95
Bufford, J.H., 46, 75
Bunting and Bernstein, 139
Burger's Hotel, 194
Buttermilk Falls, 74, 196

C

Caldwell (Mrs.) and Curella (Mrs.), 139
Cantwell and Davis, 179
Carpathian Vacation Camp, Inc., 164
Casilear, John W., 45, 71
Catskill, Village of, 24, 43, 46, 69, 72, 82, 84, 88, 93, 104, 139, 176-177
Catskill and Tannersville Railroad, 122, 184
Catskill Center for Conservation and Development, 51, 211
Catskill Mountain House, 28, 35, 39, 40, 43, 45, 46, 47, 50, 54, 55, 57, 58, 59, 61, 73, 75, 85, 88, 93, 95, 97, 98, 99, 101, 105, 106, 107, 108, 110-121, 126, 130, 133, 135, 136, 139, 142-153, 154-165, 188

219

Catskill Mountain House Company, 182
Catskill Mountain Railway (Railroad), 26, 104, 106, 107, 118, 147, 183
Catskill Mountains (geology of), 14, 175
Catskill Point, 142. *See also* Catskill, Village of
Catskill Savings Bank, 157
Catskill State Park, 140
Century Club, 43, 45
Champney, Benjamin, 68, 71
charcoal industry, 175, 180
Charles and George H. Beach and Company, 186, 188-191
The Chasm, 195
Church, Frederic E., 46, 106, 113, 211
Church's Ledge, 51, 70, 196
Cole, Maria Bartow, 72
Cole, Sarah, 45
Cole, Thomas, 20, 22, 35, 37, 38, 39, 40, 43, 44, 46, 48, 50, 51, 57, 68, 72, 99, 105, 210-213
Comfort, William, 22
Cooper, James F., 40, 92, 99, 105
Corey, Albert (Dr.), 211
Cropsey, Jasper F., 41, 42, 68, 72
Currier & Ives, 52
Curtis, George W., 101

D

Darley, Felix O.C., 27
Davis, Charles H., 29
Davis, Ebenezar, 92
Davis, S. Elmer, 172
Delisser's *Picturesque Catskills*, 46, 66, 77, 78
Dibble, Edward, 128
Dickens, Charles, 92
Dies, Jane, 82
Dimensions North, 213
Doughty, Thomas, 99

Downing, Darlene, 213
Dudley, Charles, 21
Dunn, Esther Haines, 58
Durand, Asher B., 42, 45, 48-51, 71, 76
Durham, Harvey, 178

E

Eagle Rock (South Mountain), 122, 142
East Hunter Village, 104, 176, 178, 179, 196
Elka Park, 166
Esopus Ice Company, 188
Evers, Alf, 14, 48, 76

F

Fairy Spring, 46
Family Circle and Parlor Annual, 101
Fawn's Leap, 41, 62, 64, 66, 70, 71, 73, 104, 105, 107, 192, 196
Fearon, Henry B., 92
Fenn, Harry, 54, 57
Fenner, Sears & Company, 39, 57
Field, H.S., 61
Fiero family, 114
Fisher, A.J., 61
Five Cascades, 100, 104, 196
Foster-Scott Ice Company, 188, 190
Frankel Hotel Company, 134
Fromer, Jacob, 139

G

Gardiner, Clyde, 158
Garrison, William, 209
George H. Beach and Company, 149-150
Gifford, Sanford R., 41, 43, 44, 51, 70, 136
Gillett, Edward A., 128, 132
Grant, Ulysses S. (General), 133
Greene County Historical Society, 164, 212
The Guide to Nature (Agassiz Association), 166

H

Haines, Charles ("Christian Charley"), 178
Haines Falls, Village of, 122

Haines Falls (waterfall), 14, 15, 44, 53, 56, 58, 62, 104, 106, 107, 171, 196
Haines Falls House, 201
Hall, George H., 76, 77-78, 79, 177, 194
Harding, Butler, 134
Harding, George Jr., 134
Harding, George W., 15, 126
Harper's New Monthly, 101, 105, 106
Harper's Weekly, 55, 57
Haydon, Roger, 93
Heinmann, E., 46
High Peak, 14
Hillyer's Ravine, 196
Homer, Winslow, 54, 57
Horseshoe Curve, 205
Hosmer, Harriet G., 71, 72
Hoy, Joseph J., 209
Hudson River Day Line, 80-81, 128, 135
Hudson River School of Art, 39, 76, 211-213
Hyser, Collins, 128

I
ice industry, 188-191
International Film Company, 202
Irving, Washington, 20, 33, 105

J
Jacob's Ladder, 202-208
Jefferson, Joseph, 23-25
Jensis, Annabar, 164
Johnson, David, 45, 71

K
Kaaterskill Clove Automobile Race, 198-201
Kaaterskill Clove Road, 193, 195, 197; State Highway, 202-209
Kaaterskill Creek, 14, 102, 194
Kaaterskill Falls, 14, 16, 35, 39, 40, 45, 46, 52, 54, 56, 57, 58, 59, 62, 70, 72, 75, 90, 93, 95, 96-97, 99, 101, 102, 105, 107, 125, 138, 139, 140, 141, 145, 155, 196

Kaaterskill Hotel, 15, 107, 126-135, 136, 164
Kaaterskill Post Office, 129
Kaaterskill Railroad, 133
Katz, Jacob, 14
Kensett, John F., 45, 46, 101
Kindred Spirits, 48-51
Kiskatom, 47

L
LaBelle Falls, 195
Lake Creek Bridge, 196, 200
Lane, Larry (Assemblyman), 211
Langenheim, F., et. al, 59
Laurel House, 47, 73, 75, 94, 101-102, 107, 133, 136-141, 159, 164
Layman Monument, 152
Lewis, _____, 71
Lippincott's Magazine, 105, 106
Lillie, Lucy C., 55, 106
Loeffler, J., 31, 57, 61, 64, 65, 67, 77, 119, 120, 124, 125, 137
London Stereoscopic Company, 56, 59
Lossing, Benson, 52
Lounsbury, Charles H., 166
lumbering, 175, 180, 182-187

M
Martineau, Harriet, 94-95
Mason, E.T., 62-67, 195
Mason's Cliff, 66
McCarroll, Mark, 48
McCord, Helen, 213
McEntee, Jervis, 136
Meyer, Fritz, 54, 56
Moore, Charles H., 196
Moore's Bridge, 31, 54, 104, 105, 106, 176, 194, 195, 196, 199
Morgan, W. I. (Senator), 198
Moseman, Milo C., 158-164
Motor Car Association, 201

221

The Mountain Top Historical Society, 181
Mountain Turnpike, 95, 99, 105, 194
Moynihan, Daniel P. (Senator), 213
Murdock, David (Reverend), 19
Muth, Hans, 160

N
Nast, Thomas, 54-55
National Academy of Design, 45, 75, 102
National Park Service, 211-213
Native Americans, 15, 19, 30-32, 40, 89, 106
New Hotel Palenville, 209
New York Public Library, 50
New York Herald, 134
New York State Department of Conservation, 164
New York Times, 133, 160, 162
Newman's Ledge, 93, 121
Niobe Falls, 78
North and South Lakes, 55, 73, 85, 102, 107, 108, 122, 129, 142, 145, 183, 188-190
North Mountain, 41, 42, 43, 52, 73, 93, 98, 101, 102, 107, 183
North-South Lake State Park, 135

O
Ober, George, 26
O'Connell, James (Dr.), 213
Olana, 46, 211
Onteora Park, 166
Osborn, Bloodgood, Wilbur and Fray, 149-150, 153, 156, 186, 188, 190
Otis Elevating Railway, 87, 104, 107, 118, 119, 121, 124, 125, 126, 133, 135

P
Paige, W.F., 133
Palenville, 23, 46, 48, 57, 62, 66, 68, 71, 72, 76, 78, 102, 105, 106, 107, 177, 179, 194, 200, 209
Palenville Art Colony, 46, 76

Palenville Hotel, 200
Palenville Overlook, 78, 122, 194
Palmer, Walter L., 46
Palmer Ice Company, 190
Perry, O.H., 183-187
Peters, George H., 15
Pine Orchard, 19, 30, 57, 92, 96, 99, 156, 182-187
Platte Clove (Plattekill Clove), 50
Pottery, Staffordshire, 40, 57
Power, Tyrone, 95
Profile Rock, 106, 196
Prohibition, 24, 133, 178
Prospect Mountain, 14
Prospect Rock (North Mountain), 122

Q
quarries (bluestone), 175, 179, 181, 199

R
Randolph, Hampton C., 180
Reed, Luman, 36
Reinhart, C. S., 21
Richards, Thomas A., 72, 102, 194
Rip's Lookout, 204
Rip's Retreat, 29
Rip's Rock, 27
Rip Van Winkle, 19, 20-29, 105, 106
Rip Van Winkle Bridge, 211
Rip Van Winkle Club, 24
Rip Van Winkle House, 22, 99, 105, 106, 194
Rip Van Winkle Trail, 142, 202-209
Rockwell, Charles (Reverend), 19, 105
Root, Stephen, 58, 111
Rusk, Samuel E., 16
Ruskin, John, 72

S
Santa Cruz Inn, 173
Santa Cruz Park, 166
Save America's Treasures, 213

Saxe, Ira J., 22
Schutt family (see Laurel House)
Searing, A.E.P., 53
Shelving Rock, 196
Shepard, _____, 72
Silberstein, Edith Cole, 211-213
Smith, Mabel P., 23, 29, 48, 128
South Lake boat house, 189
South Mountain, 14, 15, 40, 46, 54, 73, 101, 102, 107, 122, 126, 127, 194
Spanierman Galleries, 212
Steamboats: *Daniel Drew*, 115; *Kaaterskill*, 118; *Onteora*, 115; *Swallow* (wreck of), 83
Stereoscopic views, 58-61
Stone, Benjamin B.G., 18, 20, 25, 30, 34, 36, 46, 48, 52, 54, 58, 62, 63, 65, 68-75, 76, 80, 90, 92, 94, 106, 108, 110, 118, 126, 136, 142, 146, 154, 158, 166, 174, 176, 182, 192, 198, 202
Stony Clove, 51, 105, 147, 198
Stony Clove Railroad, 121, 128, 190
Sturgis, Jonathan, 48
Sunset Inn, 172
Sunset Rock, 57, 59, 86, 148, 151, 156, 166
Sweeny, John E. (Congressman), 213
Sylvan Lake (*see* North and South Lakes)

T
Tannenbaum, Harry, 134
Tannenbaum, Millie, 135
tanning industry, 71, 104, 176-177
Thomas Cole Foundation, 211
Thomas Cole's Cedar Grove, 40, 42, 43, 72, 164, 210-213
Towne, W. T., 61, 171
Triton's Cave, 196
Trollope, Frances, 92
Twilight Inn, 139
Twilight Park, 166, 167, 172; Ledge End Inn, 167, 170; "Tree Tops," 166-170

U
Ulster and Delaware Railroad, 122, 128, 142, 147, 190
United States Department of the Interior, 213

V
Van Gelder, James G., 121, 124
Van Gorden & Company, 84
Van Loan, Isaac, 82
Van Loan, Lucy Beach, 81, 82, 84, 88
Van Loan, Matthew Dies, 82, 83, 84
Van Loan, Petrus, 87
Van Loan, Walton, 14, 60, 66, 80-90, 194
Van Orden, Charles H., 184
Van Wagonen, John K., 134, 142, 146-158, 186
Van Wagonen, Maggie, 157
Van Wagonen, Mary L. Beach, 134, 147, 156
Van Wagonen, Virgil, 157
Van Zandt, Roland, 35, 43, 57, 76, 161, 162
Vaux, Calvert, 136
Vincent, Florence Cole Haswell, 211
Volmere, _____, 71

W
Wall, William G., 45, 54
Waltz, Joseph, 84
Ward, Jacob C., 38
Warner, Charles D., 106
Whittredge, Worthington, 43
Wild Cat Ravine, 196
Willis, Nathaniel P., 54, 99
Winthrop, Theodore, 113
Wise, Daniel, 105